IN MEMORY OF
SYLVIA TAHL KOHN
1922 - 1996

THE HOLOCAUST LIBRARY

The Death Camps

Books in the Holocaust Library

THE HOLOCAUST LIBRARY

The Death Camps

by

WILLIAM W. LACE

Lucent Books, P.O. Box 289011, San Diego, CA 92198-9011

Library of Congress Cataloging-in-Publication Data

Lace, William W.
  The death camps / by William W. Lace.
    p. cm. — (The Holocaust library)
  Includes bibliographical references and index.
  Summary: Describes the establishment of concentration camps throughout Nazi-occupied territory whose sole purpose was to exterminate Jews and other people considered undesirable by Hitler and his followers.
  ISBN 1-56006-094-8 (alk. paper)
  1. Holocaust, Jewish (1939–1945)—Juvenile literature. 2. World War, 1939–1945—Concentration camps—Juvenile literature. [1. Holocaust, Jewish (1939–1945) 2. World War, 1939–1945—Concentration camps.]
I. Title. II. Series: Holocaust library (San Diego, Calif.)
D804.34.L33 1998
940.53'18—dc21
                                                   97-36192
                                                     CIP
                                                     AC

Table of Contents

Foreword

More than eleven million innocent people, mostly Jews but also millions of others deemed "subhuman" by Adolf Hitler such as Gypsies, Russians, and Poles, were murdered by the Germans during World War II. The magnitude and unique horror of the Holocaust continues to make it a focal point in history—not only the history of modern times, but also the entire record of humankind. While the war itself temporarily changed the political landscape, the Holocaust forever changed the way we look at ourselves.

Starting with the European Renaissance in the 1400s, continuing through the Enlightenment of the 1700s, and extending to the Liberalism of the 1800s, philosophers and others developed the idea that people's intellect and reason allowed them to rise above their animal natures and conquer poverty, brutality, warfare, and all manner of evils. Given the will to do so, there was no height to which humanity might not rise. Was not mankind, these people argued, the noblest creation of God—in the words of the Bible, "a little lower than the angels"?

Western Europeans believed so heartily in these concepts that when rumors of mass murders by the Nazis began to emerge, people refused to accept—despite mounting evidence—that such things could take place. Even the Jews who were being deported to the death camps had a hard time believing that they were headed toward extermination. Rational beings, they argued, could not commit such actions. When the veil of secrecy was finally ripped from the death camps, however, the world recoiled in shock and horror. If humanity was capable of such depravity, what was its true nature? Were humans lower even than animals instead of just beneath the angels?

The perpetration of the Holocaust, so far outside the bounds of society's experience, cried out for explanations. For more than a half century, people have sought them. Thousands of books, diaries, sermons, poems, plays, films, and lectures have been devoted to almost every imaginable aspect of the Holocaust, yet it remains one of the most difficult episodes in history to understand.

Some scholars have explained the Holocaust as a uniquely German event, pointing to the racial supremacy theories of German philosophers, the rigidity of German society, and the tradition of obedience to authority. Others have seen it as a uniquely Jewish phenomenon, the culmination of centuries of anti-Semitism in Christian Europe. Still others have said that the Holocaust was a unique combination of these two factors—a set of circumstances unlikely ever to recur.

Such explanations are comfortable and simple—too simple. The Holocaust was neither a German event nor a Jewish event. It was a human event. The same forces—racism, prejudice, fanaticism—that sent millions to the gas chambers have not disappeared. If anything, they have become more evident. One cannot say, "It can't happen again." On a different scale, it has happened again. More than a million Cambodians were killed between 1974 and 1979 by a Communist government. In 1994 thousands of innocent civilians were murdered in tribal warfare between the Hutu and Tutsi tribes in the African nations of Burundi and Rwanda. Christian Serbs in Bosnia embarked on a program of "ethnic cleansing" in the mid-1990s, seeking to rid the country of Muslims.

The complete answer to the Holocaust has proved elusive. Indeed, it may never be found. The search, however, must continue. As author Elie Wiesel, a survivor of the death camps, wrote, "No one has the right to speak for the dead. . . . Still, the story had to be told. In spite of all risks, all possible misunderstandings. It needed to be told for the sake of our children."

Each book in Lucent Books' seven volume Holocaust Library covers a different topic that reveals the full gamut of human response to the Holocaust. *The Nazis*, *The Final Solution*, *The Death Camps*, and *Nazi War Criminals* focus on the perpetrators of the Holocaust and their plan to eliminate the Jewish people. Volumes on *The Righteous Gentiles*, *The Resistance*, and *The Survivors* reveal that humans are capable of being "the noblest creation of God," able to commit acts of bravery and altruism even in the most terrible circumstances.

History offers a way to interpret and reinterpret the past and an opportunity to alter the future. Lucent Books' topic-centered approach is an ideal introduction for students to study such phenomena as the Holocaust. After all, only by becoming knowledgeable about such atrocities can humanity hope to prevent future crimes from occurring. Although such historical lessons seem clear and unavoidable, as historian Yehuda Bauer wrote, "People seldom learn from history. Can we be an exception?"

Chronology of Events

1919

January 2   German Workers Party founded in Munich by Karl Harrer and Anton Drexler.

September 19   Adolf Hitler becomes member of German Workers Party.

1920

March   German Workers Party changes name to National Socialist German Workers Party, soon becomes known as Nazi Party.

1923

Fall   Hitler establishes *Stabswache*, forerunner of SS.

1929

January 6   Heinrich Himmler made head of SS.

1933

January 30   Hitler appointed chancellor of Germany.

April 7   First anti-Jewish laws passed by German Reichstag.

1935

September 13   Nuremberg Laws strip Jews of rights as citizens.

1938

November 9–10   SS mobs destroy Jewish shops and synagogues in *Kristallnacht* riots.

1939

September 1   Germany invades Poland, starting World War II.

September 21   Reinhard Heydrich orders Jews of Poland into ghettos.

October   Euthanasia program begins in Germany.

December   First use of poison gas in euthanasia center in Brandenburg, Germany.

1940

February   Labor camp for Jews established at Belzec.

February 12   Beginning of evacuation of Jews from Germany.

February 21   Concentration camp established at Auschwitz in Poland.

July   Hermann Göring assigns Heydrich plans for Final Solution; Himmler tells Rudolf Höss that Hitler has ordered the SS to carry out Final Solution.

1941

June 22   Germany invades Soviet Union; *Einsatzgruppen* begin mass killing of Communist Party officials and Jews.

July 21   Camp at Majdanek planned.

September 3   Poison gas Zyklon-B tested at Auschwitz.

October   Birkenau death camp built adjacent to Auschwitz; first gas vans tested.

November   Chelmno death camp established.

November 1   Construction begins on Belzec death camp.

December 8   Gas vans first used for killings at Chelmno.

1942

January 20 Conference at Wannsee, outside Berlin, decides on extermination as the "final solution" to the "Jewish question."

March Sobibor death camp founded.

March 7 Full-scale gassing begins at Belzec.

May 29 Heydrich fatally wounded in Czechoslovakia.

June Treblinka death camp founded.

June 13 *Sonderkommando* workers revolt in Belzec.

June 23 Full-scale gassings begin at Auschwitz.

July 19 Himmler orders all Jews in Poland to be sent to death camps by December 31.

July 23 First transports from Warsaw ghetto arrive at Treblinka.

1943

March Exhumation and cremation of bodies begins at Treblinka; Himmler orders Treblinka, Belzec, and Sobibor shut down.

July Last of Belzec prisoners removed to Sobibor.

August 19 Last gassings at Treblinka.

September 2 *Sonderkommando* workers revolt in Treblinka.

October 14 Prisoners revolt in Sobibor.

November Germans dismantle, abandon Treblinka.

December Germans dismantle, abandon Sobibor.

1944

May First shipments of Jews from Hungary arrive at Auschwitz-Birkenau.

Late July Germans abandon Chelmno, ship last prisoners to Auschwitz.

July 23 Russian troops liberate Majdanek.

October 7 Revolt of the Birkenau *Sonderkommando*.

December Last gassings at Auschwitz-Birkenau.

1945

January 6 Last executions at Auschwitz.

January 18 Germans abandon Auschwitz.

January 27 Russian troops reach Auschwitz.

May 8 German surrender ends World War II in Europe.

November 20 Top Nazis go on trial in Nuremberg.

Endlösung: The Final Solution

To Adolf Hitler, the Jews of Germany were a "problem." In his political testament, *Mein Kampf* (*My Struggle*), written nine years before the Nazi Party leader came to power in 1933, he called Jews "maggots," "blood-suckers," "vampires," "a pestilence," and "personifications of the Devil."[1] The Jews' goal, he wrote, was to defile and dilute pure German blood and take control of the world.

Hitler did not say specifically in *Mein Kampf* what should be done with the Jews, but in writing about World War I, he gave a hint:

> If, at the beginning of the War and during the War, twelve or fifteen thousand of these Hebraic [Jewish] corrupters of the nation had been subjected to poison gas such as had to be endured in the field by hundreds of thousands of our very best German workers [soldiers in World War I] . . . then the sacrifice of millions at the front would not have been in vain.[2]

On the eve of World War II, Hitler made his intentions clearer. In February 1939, he said in a speech, "Today I will once more be a prophet: if they [Jews] succeed in plunging the nations once more into a world war, then the result [will be] the anni-hilation of the Jewish race in Europe."[3]

Six months later, Hitler's troops invaded Poland and he began making his prophecy a reality. His first step was a secret euthanasia,

Heinrich Himmler (left) and Adolf Hitler direct operations against Poland in 1939. Hitler planned to annihilate the Jews.

"Mercy Killings"

In a 1929 speech Adolf Hitler said, "As a result of our modern sentimental humanitarianism we are trying to maintain the weak at the expense of the healthy." In his view, the weak, the mentally ill, and the deformed should be done away with for the health of the German nation. Ten years later, he put his opinions into practice, giving secret orders for a program of euthanasia, or "mercy killings."

This passage from *Foreign Policy, War, and Racial Extermination* by Jeremy Noakes and Geoffrey Pridham describes a scene in an asylum for children near Munich in February 1940:

> After some brief introductory remarks, Dr. [Hermann] Pfannmüller approached one of the fifteen cots which flanked the central passage to right and left. 'We have here children aged from one to five,' he pontificated. 'All these creatures represent for me as a National Socialist [Nazi] "living burdens"' . . . a burden for our nation. . . . In this sense, the Führer's [Hitler's] action to free the national community from this overburdening is quite simply a national deed, whose greatness non-medical men will only be able to assess after a period of years if not decades. We do not carry out the action with poison, injections or other measures which can be recognized . . . for then the foreign press and certain circles in Paris or London would only have new opportunities for propaganda against us. . . . No, our method is much simpler.' With these words he pulled a child out of its cot. While this fat, gross man displayed the whimpering skeletal little person like a hare which he had just caught, he coolly remarked: 'Naturally we don't stop their food straight away. That would cause too much fuss. We gradually reduce their portions. Nature then takes care of the rest. . . . This one won't last more than two or three more days.'

or mercy killing, program to "cleanse" Germany of such undesirables as the physically deformed or mentally ill. The directors of the program, Philip Bouhler and Karl Brandt, Hitler's personal physician, chose gas as the most "humane" way of killing. Bouhler hit on the idea of disguising the gas chambers as shower baths, a concept later adopted at most of the death camps.

In December 1939, the first gassing took place at a mental hospital in Brandenburg, where the medical director was Christian Wirth, later a major figure at Belzec, Sobibor, and Treblinka. Between the initial gassing and August 1941, about fifty thousand people were killed, many of whom were Jews falsely certified insane.

The *Einsatzgruppen*

On June 22, 1941, Germany invaded the Soviet Union. As Hitler's troops advanced, they were followed by another army—four

Einsatzgruppen, or action groups, many of whom were members of the *Schutzstaffel*, or protective squad. The SS, as it was known, had begun as an elite unit of bodyguards for Hitler. By the start of World War II, under its leader, *Reichsführer-SS* Heinrich Himmler, it numbered about 250,000.

The job of the *Einsatzgruppen* was to kill every Communist Party official and every Jew they could capture. A typical action involved marching victims out of a town or city, lining them up at the edge of a ravine or pit, mowing them down with machine guns, and bulldozing earth over the mass grave. In one infamous action at Babi Yar, on the outskirts of Kiev, more than 33,000 Jews were murdered. By the end of 1941, about 700,000 Jews had been killed along the eastern front.

Such massacres, however, were taking their toll on the shooters as well as the victims. In the summer of 1941, Himmler personally observed the shooting of a hundred Jews. A witness reported:

As the firing started, Himmler became more and more nervous. At each volley, he looked down at the ground. . . . [An

The Fate of the Jews

As they grew and gained power, the Nazis' policy toward the Jews seemed to go through distinct phases. At first, Jews were made second-class citizens but allowed to stay in Germany. Then, the solution was to force the Jews to leave Germany. Finally, it was decided that the Jews in Europe should be exterminated entirely.

Late in 1941 Hans Frank, governor-general of occupied Poland, issued to his staff this summary, found in *Foreign Policy, War, and Racial Extermination* by Jeremy Noakes and Geoffrey Pridham:

As for the Jews—I will be quite open with you—they will have to be finished off one way or the other. . . . I know that many of the measures now being taken against the Jews in the Reich [Germany] are criticised. It is clear from the reports on popular opinion that there are accusations of cruelty and harshness. Before I con-

tinue, I would like you to agree with me on the following principle: we are only prepared to show compassion toward the German people and to no one else on earth. . . . As an old National Socialist, I must state that if the Jewish clan were to survive the war in Europe, while we had sacrificed our best blood in the defence of Europe, then this war would only represent a partial success. With respect to the Jews, therefore, I will only operate on the assumption that they will disappear. They must go. . . . We must exterminate the Jews wherever we find them and whenever it is possible to do so in order to maintain the whole structure of the Reich here. . . . We cannot shoot these 3.5 million Jews, we cannot poison them, but we must be able to intervene in a way which somehow achieves a successful extermination.

Germans execute a group of Soviet civilians as they kneel by the side of a mass grave in 1941. During the early years of World War II, Hitler used this method to murder Jews.

SS man] addressed Himmler: *"Reichsführer,* those were only a hundred. . . . Look at the eyes of the men in this commando [team], how deeply shaken they are. These men are finished for the rest of their lives."[4]

Later that summer, Hermann Göring, Hitler's second-in-command, ordered Reinhard Heydrich, chief of the *Sicherheitsdienst* (SD), or SS security police, to prepare a detailed plan for "the final solution [*Endlösung*] of the Jewish question."[5] At about the same time, Himmler summoned Rudolf Höss, comman-

dant of the concentration camp at Auschwitz, to Berlin for instructions:

The *Führer* [Hitler] has ordered that the Jewish question be solved once and for all and that we, the SS, are to implement that order. The existing extermination centers in the east [the *Einsatzgruppen*] are not in a position to carry out the large actions which are anticipated. I have therefore earmarked Auschwitz for this purpose. . . . The Jews are the sworn enemies of the German people and must be eradicated.[6]

The *Einsatzgruppen*

The first mass murder of the Jews and other "enemies" of Germany was carried out by four military units called *Einsatzgruppen*, or action groups. Made up of police units and members of the SS, these forces followed closely behind the German army as it advanced into the Soviet Union after the invasion of June 22, 1941.

The normal procedure was to surround a town or village, usually before dawn, round up all the Communist Party officials and Jews, then march them to a secluded spot where they were gunned down and buried. In this excerpt from Noakes and Pridham's *Foreign Policy, War, and Racial Extermination*, SS officer David Ehof describes one action:

The condemned people were not only brought in lorries [trucks] but also on foot in groups of 70 or 80 persons and were mercilessly beaten in the process. The people who had been brought to the place of execution were placed about fifty metres [about 160 feet] from the graves and guarded until it was their turn to be shot. Twenty or twenty-five people at a time were led to the place of execution, to the graves. At the graves they were undressed; they even had their good quality underclothes torn from their bodies. Having been completely undressed they were driven to the graves and were forced to lie face down. The police and Germans shot them with rifles and automatic weapons. In this way more and more groups were driven to the graves and shot. They too were made to lie face down on the corpses of those who had been previously shot. At the place of execution there were snacks and schnapps [liquor]. The police drank schnapps and had a snack in the intervals between shooting the groups of Jews and then got back to their bloody work in a state of intoxication.

Members of the Einsatzkommando *pause after a mass killing of Jews.*

Shortly thereafter, Adolf Eichmann, the SS expert on Jewish affairs, visited Höss at Auschwitz. Calmly, they discussed what might be the best way of killing hundreds of thousands of people. "This could only be done by gassing," Höss wrote, "since it would have been absolutely impossible to dispose by shooting of the large numbers of people . . . and it would have placed too heavy a burden on the SS men . . . especially because of the women and children."[7]

The Six Death Camps

Although Auschwitz, along with its extermination center, Birkenau, was the largest and most infamous of the death camps, func-tionally it was by no means unique. The first extermination facility began operation in December 1941 near the Polish village of Chelmno, a short distance from the city of Lódź. In the fall of 1941, Himmler ordered Odilo Globocnik, SS commissioner in occupied Poland, to construct camps at Belzec and Sobibor near Lublin and at Treblinka near Warsaw. A sixth camp, Majdanek, had been planned near Lublin but not under Globocnik's command.

These six death camps differed fundamentally from the long-established concentration camps in Germany such as Dachau and Buchenwald. Although many thousands of people died in the latter from brutal treatment,

Jews were not the only victims of Hitler's assassination program. Here, an elderly Gypsy couple sit in an open area in Belzec concentration camp.

overwork, or disease, these camps were intended as prisons. Although two of the six death camps—Auschwitz and Majdanek—doubled as labor camps, their primary purpose was cold-blooded mass murder.

The death camps were located on major railway lines and near large cities. They were sited in Poland for three reasons. First, next to the Soviet Union, Poland had the largest concentration of Jews in Europe, about 4 million. Second, Himmler knew that such an operation could not be carried out in Germany, even under Nazi rule: Protests from church leaders and ordinary citizens had already halted the euthanasia program. Third, Poland had a long history of anti-Semitism and the Germans counted on help, not hindrance, from the local population.

The grisly work of the death camps began on December 8, 1941, with the first gassing at Chelmno and ended on January 6, 1945, with the final executions at Auschwitz. No one knows how many people were gassed, hanged, shot, beaten, worked, or simply starved to death in the camps over the three-year period. Estimates range as high as 4 million.

By any measure, the greatest crime in the history of the world occurred in the death camps. Half a century later, it is difficult to comprehend its enormity. Indeed, some people insist—despite physical evidence and the testimony of eyewitnesses—that the Holocaust never happened. As one SS guard said when asked if he was worried about world reaction to the death camps, "They would not believe you. They'd say you were mad. . . . How can anyone believe this terrible business—unless he has lived through it?"[8]

1 *Begrüsung:* The Welcome

The misery of millions of Jews and other victims of the Nazi death camps began long before they reached the camps themselves. Their journey, whether of a few or a few hundred miles, was one of almost indescribable suffering. Many did not survive. Only death—or an existence perhaps worse than death—awaited those who did.

Before they were shipped to the death camps, most Jews were first concentrated in ghettos. Uprooted from their countryside and village homes, they were forced to relocate to the larger cities of Poland. There, they were packed with their urban counterparts into sections of the city sealed off with walls and barbed wire. Living quarters were terribly overcrowded. Food was scarce. Sanitation was impossible. Hundreds died each day.

The Germans, citing the wretched conditions they themselves had caused, ordered the ghettos' Jewish councils—the *Judenräte*—to select those who would be sent for "resettlement" to labor camps. Deportees were told to bring their valuables and their best tools. In the early months, before rumors of the death camps spread, many volunteered.

Jews gathered for transport at a central point, which was then surrounded by armed guards and attack dogs. After a wait—sometimes an entire day—a locomotive appeared, pulling not passenger cars but wooden cattle cars. Abraham Goldfarb, a survivor of Treblinka, remembered that "the Germans forced 150–200 [Jews] into a freight car designed for sixty or seventy. The cars were closed from the outside with boards. Water and food were not provided."[9] In demanding payment from the SS for its services, the German railway system conceded that these were "special" trains and agreed to accept a group or "excursion" fare.

The journey from the Polish ghettos to the death camps was supposed to take only a few hours. Often, however, trains were routinely rerouted or delayed and a fifty-mile trip took three days. Conditions inside the cars were appalling. Abraham Kszepicki described his journey to Treblinka:

> It is impossible to describe the tragic situation in our airless, closed freight car. It was one big toilet. Everyone tried to push his way to a small air aperture. . . . I found a crack in one of the floorboards into which I pushed my nose in order to get a little air. The stink in the car was unbearable. People were defecating in all four corners of the car. . . . The men removed their shirts and lay half naked. Some of the women, too, took off their dresses and lay in their undergarments. People lay on the floor, gasping and

In 1941, Jewish deportees from the Lódź ghetto are transferred from a closed passenger train to open cars on their way to the Chelmno death camp. The Germans used every means possible to prevent the Jews from finding out they were on their way to being executed.

shuddering as if feverish, laboring to get some air into their lungs.[10]

Tortured by Thirst

Hunger was not the greatest problem. Many people brought sausages, bread, and fruit with them and were willing to share. But thirst was another matter, especially in the summer when the sun beat down on the closed boxcars. "The children were so thirsty," said Goldfarb, "that they licked their mothers' sweat."[11] The Jews begged water from the SS guards and railway workers. Sometimes, they received a drink out of kindness. More often, it was sold to them at exorbitant prices.

In the winter, when the trains stopped at stations, those inside the cars would implore the people outside to throw them some snow. "The lucky ones, who had caught the snow, fell upon it like madmen," wrote Salmen Gradowski of a train to Auschwitz. "They quarrel and scuffle about each piece, they raise from the floor crumbs which fell due to carelessness."[12]

Diseases rampant in the ghettos were carried onto the trains. There was no way to isolate the sick. "The only quarantine we could enforce was to have those who were near the infected ones turn their backs," wrote physician Olga Lengyel. When the first person aboard her car died, the dead

Life in the Ghetto

Before they were shipped to the death camps, the Jews of Poland were rounded up and packed inside ghettos, sealed-off sections of selected Polish cities. Here, in terribly crowded, unsanitary conditions, they lived as best they could. In 1940 a Polish Christian, Stanislaw Rozycki, visited the ghetto in Warsaw. His description is found in *Foreign Policy, War, and Racial Extermination* by Jeremy Noakes and Geoffrey Pridham:

> The majority are nightmare figures, ghosts of former human beings, miserable destitutes, pathetic remnants of former humanity. One is most affected by the characteristic change which one sees in their faces: as a result of misery, poor nourishment, the lack of vitamins, fresh air and exercise, the numerous cares, worries, and anticipated misfortunes, suffering and sickness, their faces have taken on a skeletal appearance. The prominent bones around their eye sockets, the yellow facial colour, the slack pendulous skin, the alarming emaciation and sickliness. And, in addition, this miserable, frightened, restless, apathetic and resigned expression like that of a hunted animal. I pass my closest friends without recognising them and guessing their fate. Many of them recognise me, come up to me and ask curiously how things are "over there" behind the walls—there where there is enough bread, fresh air, freedom to move around, and above all freedom. On the streets children are crying in vain, children who are dying of hunger. They howl, beg, sing, moan, shiver with cold, without underwear, without clothing, without shoes, in rags, sacks, flannel which are bound in strips round the emaciated skeletons, children swollen with hunger, disfigured, half conscious, already completely grown-up at the age of five, gloomy and weary of life. They are like old people and are only conscious of one thing: "I'm cold." "I'm hungry."

man's son shouted to a guard, "We have a corpse in our midst!" The guard shouted back, "Keep your corpse. You will have many more of them soon."[13]

Pregnant women had to give birth on dirty blankets. More often than not, neither mothers nor babies survived the journey. Former prisoner Tadeusz Borowski wrote that when his train arrived at Auschwitz, "amid human excrement . . . lie squashed, trampled infants, naked little monsters with enormous heads and bloated bellies."[14]

The doors of the cars were occasionally opened, but more often for robbery than relief. One guard stuck his head into Lengyel's car and announced, "Thirty wristwatches, right away. If not, you may all consider yourselves dead."[15] A survivor of Sobibor, Ada Lichman, wrote, "Soldiers entered the cars and robbed us and even cut off fingers with rings. They claimed we didn't need them any more."[16]

Journeys to Death

When the Nazis began transporting Jews from western Europe, the journeys—at least in the early months—were not as terrible. The Jews who had been forced to pay exorbitant fares, got to ride in passenger cars. They were permitted to get off the trains at stations along the way and to buy food. Later in the war, however, the Jews of France, Belgium, and Holland were, like their eastern counterparts, jammed into boxcars and had to suffer journeys on which days became weeks. On arrival at the death camps, the dead frequently outnumbered the living. One trip, from northwestern Greece, lasted twenty-eight days. When the guards opened the car doors at Auschwitz, they found only corpses.

In 1943 the Germans largely abandoned the pretense of telling their victims they were going to labor camps and sometimes forced the Jews to climb aboard the cars naked to increase the difficulty of escape. One transport from Lvov was sent to Belzec in the dead of winter. Belzec, however, was in the process of shutting down, so the train was diverted to Sobibor. By the time it arrived, a Sobibor prisoner said, "the corpses were frozen and stuck to one another, and when they were laid on the trolley, they disintegrated, and parts of them fell off. These people had had a long journey and their corpses crumbled." [17]

As the trains neared the death camps, alert passengers were given grim hints as to what lay ahead. They did not know where they were headed, but the local population did. Salmen Gradowski saw two women weeping at the sight of his train and making the sign of the cross. Other signs were more ominous. Some of the Polish bystanders drew their fingers across their throats or pointed to the ground. Samuel Willenberg heard one man shout, "Jews, they are going to make you into soap." [18]

When the trains at last reached their destinations, more rude shocks awaited those onboard. Christian Wirth, who had moved most of his euthanasia team from Germany and was now commandant of Belzec, had established two basic principles for handling the arrival of transports. First, maintain at any cost the fiction that the victims had arrived at a labor camp, not an extermination facility.

At Belzec, the unloading platform was made to look like an ordinary country railway station. Flowers and shrubs were planted. At Auschwitz-Birkenau, a small orchestra played show tunes. Timetables were posted by a ticket office. Doors bore

Prisoners arrive at Auschwitz in 1944. Crematory chimneys can be seen at the right and left of the photo.

signs reading First Class, Waiting Room, and Cashier. Another large sign bore a directional arrow and the name of the next town. In reality, this was—in every way—the end of the line. So convincing was the hoax that "some people from the transport turned to us workers of the so-called 'station commando' [prisoners who unloaded the trains] and offered us tips to help them carry their luggage."[19]

Signs at Belzec read:

Attention Warsaw Jews!
You are now entering a transit camp from which you will be transported to a labour camp. To prevent epidemics both clothing and luggage must be handed in for disinfecting. Gold, cash, foreign exchange [money], and jewelry are to be given up at the cash desk in return for a receipt. They will be later returned on presentation of the receipt. All those arriving must cleanse themselves by taking a bath before continuing their journey.[20]

Unsettling Sights

Less reassuring was the sight of the SS men on the platform. An Auschwitz survivor recalled "beefy men with highly polished boots and shiny, brutal faces. Some have brought their briefcases, others hold thin, flexible whips."[21] Also disturbing was the appearance of the musicians, whose sprightly tunes seemed strange when played by men in striped prison uniforms. Then, too, there were the prisoners who helped the newcomers down from the cars and took their luggage. They were thin, pale, and looked alarmingly unhealthy. "We meet people whose appearance is horrifying,"[22] wrote Gradowski.

When the death camps were in full operation, even more ominous sights and smells greeted newcomers. "No one who came out alive of a German execution camp can ever forget the picture that greeted us at Auschwitz," wrote physician Gisella Perl. "Like big, black clouds, the smoke of the crematory hung over the camp. Sharp red tongues of flame licked the sky, and the air was full of the nauseating smell of burning flesh."[23] Another Auschwitz doctor, Miklos Nyiszli, remembered, "I tried to realize what hellish cooking would require such a tremendous fire. . . . A faint wind brought the smoke toward me. My nose, then my throat were filled with the nauseating odor of burning flesh and scorched hair."[24]

Wirth's second principle was that new arrivals should be given as little time as possible to reflect on their surroundings. Commandant Höss of Auschwitz wrote that "the whole business of arriving and undressing should take place in an atmosphere of the greatest possible calm."[25] In practice, what actually took place was anything but calm. At the moment the cars ground to a stop, SS men and members of the *Bahnhofkommando*, or "platform team" of prisoners, began beating on the sides with clubs and rifle butts. Adding to the clamor were fierce police dogs, barking and straining at the leashes held by their handlers.

The Jews stumbled from the cars, their eyes blinded either by the daylight or by bright spotlights. Shouts of *"Schnell! Schnell!"*—"Faster! Faster!"—filled the air. Those who stumbled or did not move fast enough were whipped or clubbed. The new arrivals were separated into two groups, women and children in one, men and older boys in the other. They were pushed and shoved into ranks of five, a favorite formation in the death camps. At Auschwitz, a dwarf in an SS uniform ran among them,

Checking In

If people arriving in the death camps from the ghettos had any hope they had been taken to a better place, that hope soon was shattered. If they were lucky enough to be selected for work, this is the type of reception they received, taken from the record of an anonymous prisoner and reprinted in *Majdanek* by Czeslaw Rajca and Anna Wisniewska:

> At the entrance, everybody got a piece of metal sheet with a number imprinted on it. They warned us straight away we had to take good care of it, for in case it got lost, one was to be flogged twenty five strokes the first time, fifty the second, and shot the third time. . . . Each was given a cloth star. It was made up of two triangles, yellow and red. The yellow meant we were Jewish, and the red politically suspected. . . . Our shoes were taken away and wooden clogs given instead. I happened upon clogs size 44 (my size being 40) because they only had them that large. It was difficult moving with those on. Then we proceeded to have medical examinations. . . . Some got certificates; I got one saying I had something broken. It was of no use to me, this paper, for they detailed me to work with coal, which was one of the heaviest jobs. I tried to protest, quoting the certificate. In return, I suffered several blows on the head with a horsewhip. After the examination was over, we were driven to the bathhouse. We stripped off the clothes and went over to have a haircut and shave. There were large tubs with water there. Inmates washed in them, one by one. In the same water, never changed, many people had a wash. Who knows how many there might have been before me and how many more there were going to be after.

beating them with a club. In the early days of the camps, before special rooms for undressing were built, prisoners were made to strip and leave their clothes on the ground. The entire scene—the pretty station, the distant chimneys, the music of the orchestra, the dogs barking, the SS shouting—was one of total chaos and unreality.

"Medical" Treatment

Ambulances bearing red crosses pulled up alongside the trains. "We were told that these would transport the ailing," wrote Lengyel. "Another good sign! . . . We could not possibly have guessed that the ambulances would cart the sick directly to the gas chambers."[26] At Sobibor the sick, told they would be given medical treatment, were taken to the lazarette, or hospital. There they were killed by gunshot or by lethal injection. Some were taken alive out a back door and carted directly to the pits where bodies were being cremated, then shot and thrown to the flames.

Once the cars were cleared of all who could walk, the workers removed the sick and the dead. Sometimes, it was hard to tell the difference. At Sobibor, prisoner Dov Freiberg laid a corpse on the ground beside others: "And then the body, which I thought was of a dead man, rose up, looked at me with great eyes and asked: 'Is it still far?'"[27] Under the whip of an SS man, Freiberg loaded the still-living man on a trolley to be carried to the crematory.

While those able to walk stood in formation, the Germans continued to offer false reassurance. Filip Müller remembered an SS sergeant at Auschwitz who asked a man his trade. A tailor, he was told. "That's precisely the sort of people we need in our workrooms," the German replied. "When you've had your shower, report to me at once."[28] At Sobibor, Sergeant Hermann Michel told those about to die that "it was time for Jews to become a productive element. At present all of them would be going to the Ukraine to live and work. This address aroused confidence and enthusiasm among the people. They applauded spontaneously and sometimes even danced and sang."[29]

As rumors of the death camps spread, the Germans sometimes went to extraordinary lengths to deceive their victims. Müller wrote of one Auschwitz transport whose passengers were convinced they were being taken to Switzerland and had deboarded at the Swiss border. An SS officer introduced a member of the German Foreign Office, who told the crowd assembled on a platform hundreds of miles to the east in Poland, "We have brought you here because the Swiss authorities insist that each one of you must be disinfected before you cross the frontier."[30] Trusting the "official," actually an SS officer in civilian clothes, the prisoners went calmly to their deaths.

When the groups were in formation, it was time for the selection. Each rank was led before an SS officer, usually a doctor. Often presiding at Auschwitz was the notorious Josef Mengele, one of several Nazi physicians who performed bizarre experiments on prisoners. The task of the selection officer was to determine who would die and who would be kept alive—for a while, at least—to work.

The Rule of Selection

In the early months of the death camps, when slave labor was needed to complete and expand the camps, all women and children were killed, but most of the able-bodied men were spared for work. Later, women were chosen to work as cooks, maids for the SS, and in the laundries. Skilled carpenters and

The sadistic German physician Josef Mengele. Mengele met prisoners upon their arrival, deciding who would live and who would die.

Writing Home

The Germans used every possible device to deceive death camp newcomers into thinking they had been taken to a labor camp instead. One such deception—the writing of postcards—was intended to fool not only the prisoners, but also those they had left behind.

In *Five Chimneys*, Olga Lengyel recalled that two days after her arrival she and other inmates were permitted to write postcards to their relatives back home. The postcards were all to say that the writers were in good health in a labor camp in Waldsee in Germany, not in Auschwitz. Lengyel wrote:

> Only in August did I understand why the German authorities had encouraged this correspondence. A new train had arrived at Auschwitz-Birkenau, and many deportees confided that the good news they had received from the camp while they were still at home had reassured them and made them neglect certain precautions that might have spared them deportation. Others stated that the cards our internees had addressed to them had given away their whereabouts to the German authorities.

Petro Mirchuk, in *In the German Mills of Death*, reported that once a month each prisoner was allowed to write an eleven-line letter beginning with, "I am well and everything is fine." Mirchuk added that incoming prisoners were made to write similar letters assuring others that they were well, that the work was hard but they were paid wages, and that they were being allowed to live with their families in clean quarters. Such letters were postdated by several months. "For instance," Mirchuk wrote, "if a prisoner were brought in during January, 1943, his letter would be dated March or April, 1943, long after he would have been gassed."

electricians stood a good chance of staying alive. So did doctors and nurses. The general rule was that children under age fourteen, men over fifty, and women over forty-five were exterminated.

Regardless of their age, women with small children were usually sent to the gas chambers: The SS did not want to go to the trouble of parting them. Later, the Germans decided that children under five were harder to kill with gas than adults. Children, therefore, were taken from their mothers directly to the crematoria. There, wrote Petro Mirchuk, a member of the Auschwitz *Sonderkommando*, or special team of prisoners whose task it was to drag bodies from the gas chambers to the ovens or cremation pits, "they were undressed and pushed into the fire. After a few minutes of extremely high heat, there would remain only an ash where there had been a child."[31] The Germans wasted not even a bullet on them.

The number selected for work depended on the frequency and size of the transports and the current labor demand. At Auschwitz and Majdanek, which provided labor for

Prisoners at work in Majdanek concentration camp. Much of the work performed by inmates was useless physical labor made to tax their bodies and souls.

nearby factories, as little as 40 percent to an average of 80 percent of a transport was exterminated. The percentage was higher in the other camps, which needed only enough labor for the camps themselves. In 1944, when masses of Jews were brought from Hungary to Auschwitz, the extermination rate approached 100 percent.

As the transportees were led before the selection officer, he studied each person for a few seconds and then directed them either to the left or to the right. To the left were the gas chambers; to the right was work. While most SS doctors considered these selections the hardest part of their duties— Hans Köning of Auschwitz prepared for his turn by getting drunk—Mengele seemed to relish them. Wearing a tight, black SS uni-

form with white gloves and whistling tunes from operas, he would point his cane at each person and, with a flick of his wrist, send him or her toward life or death.

Whispered Advice

In rare instances, workers would try to warn victims, whispering advice about what to tell the selection officer. Elie Wiesel was asked how old he was. Fifteen, he answered. "No," insisted the prisoner. "Eighteen." Wiesel protested that he was only fifteen. "Fool," hissed the prisoner. "Listen to what *I* say."[32] Wiesel lied to the selection officer and was saved.

Others were not so lucky. Olga Lengyel hurriedly surmised that those sent to the left would be cared for and spared any hard labor. Her son Arvad was big for his age, but his mother insisted to the selection officer that he was only twelve. "Very well," the officer said. "To the left."[33] She had condemned her own son to the gas chamber.

The prisoners had little incentive to warn the victims. In all likelihood a prisoner spared death on arrival would die eventually anyway. In addition, their muttered advice was not often believed. Lengyel tried to warn some women to lie to the selection officer. "They asked, 'Why?' and looked at me as though to say, What does this dirty woman want. She must be mad."[34] More-

over, if caught, prisoners would be punished swiftly and severely. In 1943 a worker recognized a friend's wife and told her the group was to be gassed. He was overheard, taken to one of the crematoria, and burned alive.

Despite the brutality of the SS and the stink of the crematoria, some of the victims still refused to believe that such places as the death camps could exist. They believed in a world of law, fairness, and decency, never dreaming that that world lay far behind them. A lawyer rushed up to an SS officer to protest that a guard was killing innocent

At Auschwitz in 1944, young prisoners arrive and receive a blanket before going to the barracks. Their smiles and calm belie that they knew little of what was to come.

people. The officer summoned the guard and told him to give the lawyer what he deserved. The lawyer was beaten to death. The officer surveyed the crowd and said, "Anyone else want to make a complaint?"[35]

The selection ended with those chosen for work being led off in one direction, those condemned to death in another. The dead and the sick were taken directly to the fires. Mountains of luggage and piles of clothing remained behind. Victims sometimes tried to hide in the piles. At Treblinka, one naked prisoner managed to burrow among the clothing, dress himself, and mingle with the workers. Others were not so lucky. SS sergeant Pery Broad wrote, "A child's thin wailing was sometimes heard from under a bundle of clothing. . . . The child would then be lifted, held aloft and shot through the head by some utterly bestial hangman."[36]

Human Residue

When all the people had dispersed, disposal of their belongings commenced. Clothing was sorted by the *Lumpenkommando* for later shipment to Germany. It would be washed—bloodstains were especially hard to remove—

Piles of clothing at Dachau reveal the huge number of people who gave up their lives in the camp.

After liberation women use the boots of the dead as fuel for a cooking fire at the camp at Belsen. These piles of clothing are mute testimony to the many who lost their lives there.

and any identifying name tags and labels would be cut out, including the yellow Stars of David the Jews had been forced to wear in the ghettos.

Specially trained teams of *Goldjuden*, or "gold Jews," sorted through all the valuables that had been surrendered. Willenberg reported that the average daily haul in Treblinka amounted to "kilograms of gold and diamonds, thousands of gold watches, and millions of coins from all over the world, including China."[37] In 1944, Globocnik submitted a report detailing seizures at Treblinka, Belzec, and Sobibor while they were

in operation. The total—seven thousand pounds of gold, fifty thousand pounds of silver, sixteen thousand carats of diamonds, and money from forty-eight countries—was worth more than $7 million in 1944.

Personal items—birth certificates, diaries, diplomas, family photographs—were burned. The Germans wanted to destroy not only the Jews, but any indication they had come to the death camps. "No name is to ever leave this place,"[38] the foreman of a *Lumpenkommando* told his clothes-sorting crew.

A large share of the plunder went not to Germany, but into the pockets of the SS.

Despite dire threats from Berlin of courts-martial and even executions, officers and guards helped themselves to fine foods and expensive clothes in addition to money and jewels. Items worth hundreds of dollars, smuggled out of the sorting yard by prisoners who risked death if they were caught, would be traded to a guard for a sausage or a pack of cigarettes. "I think they all became millionaires in Treblinka,"[39] wrote Willenberg of the SS. The wife and children of Commandant Höss wore silk underwear they could never have otherwise afforded, brought to Auschwitz by Jews soon to die.

Month after month, the Jews of Europe were shipped to the death camps. In only a few, frantic minutes, their clothes, their cherished belongings, and any last illusions were stripped away. Within hours the Germans would take the lives of most of them and attempt to take the dignity and souls of the rest.

Sonderbehandlung:
Special Handling

Killing people—millions of people—was the primary business of the death camps. As in any large, novel operation, there were mistakes, experiments, and refinements until, at last, the machinery ran with a practiced, murderous efficiency. And, as in other industries, there were troublesome by-products whose disposal presented a major problem. In this case, the by-products were bodies.

Although the Germans had decided that the best method of slaughtering the Jews (the code word used in official documents was *Sonderbehandlung*, or special handling) was poison gas, shootings still took place. Transports sometimes came by truck instead of train, and shooting was the preferred technique if the victims numbered fewer than two hundred. At Sobibor, they would be taken to the lazarette, supposedly for medical treatment. At Auschwitz, they were led to Block 11, the building for torture and punishment. There, they were dragged before a wall made of black cork. Then, Filip Müller wrote,

As on the production line of a slaughterhouse, members of the SS . . . put them to death with a shot through the base of the skull from their silenced small-bore rifles. . . . Before the next batch was let

in, the floor was hosed down. Sometimes things became so hectic that we had no time to remove all traces of blood. And the wretched victims had to stand in the blood of those who had preceded them.[40]

Late in the war, when ammunition became scarce, the Germans used guns powered by springs that drove needles into the base of the victim's brain. Such guns were normally used to kill cattle.

Poison gas, however, was the method of choice. The questions were, What kind of gas? and, How was it to be administered? The euthanasia centers in Germany had used cylinders of carbon monoxide, much too expensive and difficult to transport for an enterprise as large as the Final Solution. In September 1941, the first experiments using ordinary motor vehicle exhaust fumes piped into sealed rooms were carried out in the Soviet Union. Reinhard Heydrich devised a mobile version of this execution chamber; he ordered special vans built in which the exhaust fumes would be piped into the rear compartment, killing all the occupants.

Chelmno

The vans were tested in October and delivered to the *Einsatzgruppen* in the Soviet

The mobile killing van used to gas Jews as they were transported to the mass graves at Chelmno. The vans were abandoned because they took too long to asphyxiate their captives.

Union. They were such a success that the next month they were put into use at Chelmno, the first of the death camps.

Chelmno was unlike any of the other camps. There were no huge trainloads of victims, only truckloads. The Jews were brought to a large home in the country—the Mansion—and told they were to be disinfected before being sent on to work camps. After undressing, they were hustled along a passage and packed—thirty-five or forty at a time—into the backs of trucks nicknamed "ghetto autobuses" by the SS. The doors were sealed and the trucks drove off. One of the drivers, Gustav Laabs, remembered the end of the journey: "After about three kilometers we drove into a clearing in the forest. . . . Some of the work detail were then ordered to open the rear doors. After this had been done 9–10 bodies fell out of the van onto the ground."[41]

The bodies were thrown into pits, layered with calcium oxide, or quicklime, to speed decomposition, and covered with earth. Compared to what would occur elsewhere, the procedure was primitive. Sometimes, not everyone in the van would be dead when the grave was reached. On several occasions, frantic Jews succeeded in breaking open the sides of the van. Chelmno was the least "productive" of the death camps. Still, about 152,000 people died there.

Clearly, larger, more permanent gassing facilities were needed. The first gas chambers were built at Belzec by Christian Wirth, formerly of the Brandenburg euthanasia program.

Wirth's building contained three rectangular rooms, each about thirteen by twenty-six feet, with ceilings just over six feet high. A 250-horsepower engine from a captured Russian tank was installed in a shed just outside, and exhaust fumes were piped into the chambers. The gas chambers at Sobibor and Treblinka followed the same blueprint.

The look on this man's face seems to register resignation as he waits, with other Jewish men, to be gassed in the mobile van at Chelmno death camp.

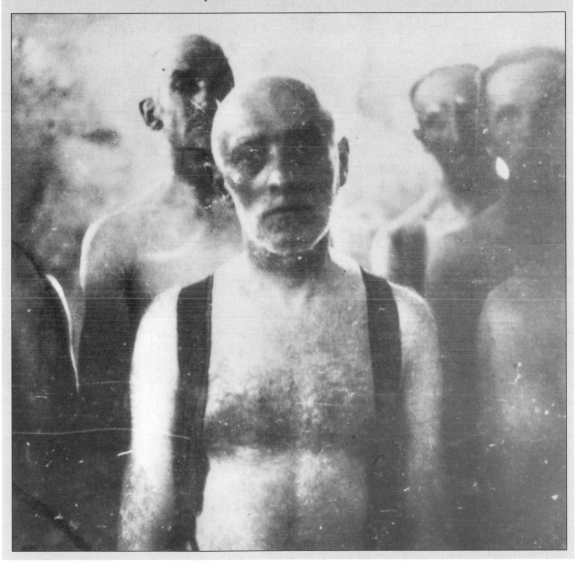

Breakdown

Eventually, the death camps functioned all too efficiently. In the early months, however, while the Germans searched for a perfect way to dispose of millions of people, this was not always the case. The euthanasia program in Germany had used cylinders of carbon monoxide gas, too expensive for the death camps. Instead, internal combustion engines were used. They were not always effective, as shown in this excerpt from *Belzec, Sobibor, Treblinka,* by Yitzhak Arad. From a report by SS colonel Kurt Gerstein:

Unterscharführer [Sergeant] Hackenholt was making great efforts to get the engine running. But it doesn't go. Captain [Christian] Wirth comes up. I can see he is afraid because I am present at a disaster. Yes, I see it all and I wait. My stopwatch showed it all, 50 minutes, 70 minutes, and the diesel did not start. The people wait inside the gas chambers. In vain. They can be heard weeping, "like in a synagogue," says Professor [Hermann] Pfannensteil, his eyes glued to a window in the wooden door. Furious, Captain Wirth lashes the Ukrainian assisting Hackenholt twelve, thirteen times in the face. After 2 hours and 49 minutes—the stopwatch recorded it all—the diesel started. Up to that moment, the people shut up in those four crowded chambers were alive, four times 750 persons in four times 45 cubic meters. Another 25 minutes elapsed. Many were already dead; that could be seen through the small window because an electric lamp inside lit up the chamber for a few moments. After 28 minutes, only a few were still alive. Finally, after 32 minutes, all were dead.

Meanwhile, Höss was planning the extermination facility at Birkenau, next to Auschwitz. He considered gassing by carbon monoxide unreliable. The engines kept breaking down, and the uneven distribution of the gas left some people still alive when the doors were opened. Höss needed a more convenient, more reliable gas.

Zyklon-B

As it happened, such a gas was already to be found at Auschwitz. Zyklon-B, greenish crystalline pellets that released lethal hydrogen cyanide gas when exposed to air, was being used at Auschwitz as a pesticide for the fumigation of buildings crawling with lice and rats. On September 3, 1941, Höss's deputy, Karl Fritsch, conducted an experiment. He crammed Russian prisoners into the cells of Block 11, hurled Zyklon-B pellets inside, and slammed the doors. "In the crowded cells, death came instantaneously the moment the Zyklon-B was thrown in," Höss wrote about an experiment he witnessed later that month. "A short, almost smothered cry, and it was all over."[42]

Höss liked to boast that his camp was the home of Zyklon-B, which also came to be used in the gas chambers at Majdanek. He constantly belittled the carbon monoxide method to Eichmann and Himmler. Wirth just as stoutly resisted any change in the combustion engine technique he had developed in the euthanasia centers and at Belzec. He sneeringly referred to Höss as "my untalented disciple."[43]

For the Jews, the two kinds of gas amounted to the same thing—an agonizing death. After a selection, those marked for gassing were led away. At Auschwitz, and later at all the camps, they were taken to changing rooms, the walls of which bore signs such as "Cleanliness Brings Freedom" and "One Louse Can Kill You."[44] Victims disrobed and hung their clothes on numbered pegs. Guards told them to be sure to remember their number so they could find their clothes after their baths.

Two German workers at Majdanek death camp display canisters of Zyklon-B used in the gas chambers.

Filip Müller heard a little girl in the Auschwitz changing room ask, "Mummy, why are we undressing? . . . Is the doctor going to examine me, and make me well again?" "He will, my darling," replied the mother, who had once lived near the camp and knew full well what was to happen. "Soon you will be well, and then we'll all be happy."[45]

Pathway to Death

Before changing rooms were built, the victims were hustled naked along a path to the gas chambers, leaving their clothes in the reception area. In Sobibor and Belzec, the path was called the *Schlauch*, or tube. In Treblinka, the SS derisively nicknamed it the *Himmelstrasse*, or road to heaven. Although many must have suspected they were not headed for baths, the Germans kept up the pretense. At Treblinka, guards would shout, "Faster! Faster! The water's getting cold."[46] At Belzec, guards advised the victims, "Just breathe deeply in the chambers. It will strengthen your lungs."[47]

Finally, the victims were tightly packed into the gas chambers—men first, then women. Sometimes, when small children were gassed, they were thrown in on top of the adults. When the door was slammed shut and the lights turned off, panicked people began screaming and pounding on the walls. This frenzy was allowed to go on for several minutes: The ever-efficient SS had discovered the gas was more effective if the victims' body heat raised the chamber temperature.

Guards then activated the gas, either by starting the internal combustion engines or by pouring Zyklon-B into the chambers. At Auschwitz-Birkenau, "medical personnel" in white coats and gas masks climbed onto the roof, where special openings led down into the chambers. Sergeant-Major Otto Moll gave the signal by shouting, "*Na, gib ihnen schon zu fressen*"—"Now, let them eat

Some Fast Talking

Perhaps the quickest thinker and smoothest liar in all of the Nazi death camps was SS captain Franz Hössler, whose job it was to calm the fears of Jews when they arrived at Auschwitz. It was Hössler's task to convince them they were in a labor camp. Filip Müller recalls portions of Hössler's speeches in *Eyewitness Auschwitz:*

> On behalf of the camp administration I bid you welcome. This is not a holiday resort but a labour camp. . . . How you tackle this task is entirely up to you. The chance is there for every one of you. We shall look after your health and we shall offer you well-paid work. . . . Oh, yes, before I forget, after your bath, please have ready your indentures [identification papers], diplomas, school reports and any other documents so that we can employ everybody according to his or her training and ability. Would diabetics who are not allowed sugar report to staff on duty after their baths.

The "bath," of course, was death in the gas chamber.

Occasionally, prisoners would try to incite their comrades to rebellion. On one such occasion, Hössler had to do some fast talking:

> Ladies and gentlemen! What in heaven's name has got into you. I've read the [commandant's] report, and according to that the authorities appear to have been quite happy with the behavior of you Jews in the ghettos. . . . Living conditions here are much better. But in return we do expect discipline. . . . Surely you're not going to listen to a lunatic? On the other hand, if you don't obey our orders, we'll have to take that as a refusal to work, with serious consequences for you, I'm afraid. Refusing to obey orders really doesn't pay. There's a war on, and everybody must do his or her duty.

it."[48] The blue-green crystals were poured through the openings and into hollow perforated pillars through which the gas seeped into the room.

The victims tried to distance themselves from the pillars, clawing at one another and climbing over the backs of their fellows. Their screams turned to coughs as the gas penetrated their lungs and they fought to breathe. People began to fall and die. Sometimes, they were wedged together so tightly that there was no room to fall. As an SS man watched through a peephole, movement gradually slowed and then stopped. After about twenty minutes, it was all over and exhaust fans began pumping gas out of the chamber.

"Now," wrote an Auschwitz-Birkenau survivor, "a real hell begins."[49] The bodies, streaked with blood from the victims' struggles and with excrement from bowels loosened in the final agony of asphyxiation, had to be hosed down. This also neutralized any remaining Zyklon-B crystals. Then *Sonderkommando* workers, under the whips of the SS and Ukrainian guards, began sorting out the tangle of arms and legs, slipping leather straps around the wrists of the bodies to drag them off for burial or cremation.

Final Indignities

Before going to the pits or flames, however, the corpses were subjected to a series of final indignities. Women's hair was cut off if it had not already been cut, as in Sobibor and Treblinka. In Auschwitz-Birkenau, the hair was dried on clotheslines in the oven rooms, combed out, and shipped to Germany to be made into industrial thread and felt for the insulation of submarines. Body openings were searched for hidden valuables. Workers known as "dentists" pried open mouths and wrenched gold teeth from their sockets with pliers. The gold was melted, molded into ingots, and sent to Berlin. Only after every possible economic contribution to the Third Reich had been made was the corpse disposed of.

In the early days of the death camps, bodies were buried in huge pits similar to those dug by the *Einsatzgruppen* in Russia. The results horrified even the SS. Treblinka commandant Franz Stangl, visiting Belzec, saw that "one of the pits had overflowed.

No one who looks at this tragic photo can remain unmoved at the evil that humans can perpetrate on one another. This huge grave at Belsen shows the bodies of political prisoners who were starved and mistreated until death came as a welcome release.

They had put too many corpses in it and putrefaction had progressed too fast so that the liquid underneath had pushed the bodies on top up and over, and the corpses had rolled down the hill. I saw some of them—oh God, it was awful."[50] At Auschwitz-Birkenau, "a black, evil-smelling mass oozed out and polluted the ground water in the vicinity."[51]

The situation was so bad that in the spring of 1942 Himmler ordered the corpses dug up and burned. He did so for reasons of secrecy as well as sanitation: Himmler wanted to erase all evidence of the mass murders.

The Germans first tried opening the pits and blowing up the bodies with explosives, but the blasts only scattered the remains. Then they tried pouring fuel on the bodies and setting them on fire, but there was not enough oxygen in the bottom of the pits to sustain combustion and only the top layer burned. Finally, the rotting bodies had to be dug up either by the *Sonderkommando* or with steam shovels. Samuel Willenberg saw bodies and parts of bodies falling from the giant scoops.

The "Roaster"

Huge grills were built using railroad rails, lighter trolley rails being unable to withstand the intense heat. Corpses were stacked on the grill, called a "roaster" in Sobibor, and set on fire. Treblinka survivor Yechiel Reichmann described how the SS made a science out of the burnings:

The SS "expert" on bodyburning ordered us to put women, particularly fat women [to act as fuel], on the first layer of the grill, face down. The second layer could consist of whatever was brought—men, women, or children—and so on, layer on top of layer. Then the "expert"

ordered us to lay dry branches under the grill and to light them. Within a few minutes the fire would take so it was difficult to approach the crematorium from as far away as 50 meters [about 162 feet] away. . . . The work was extremely difficult. The stench was awful. Liquid excretions from the corpses squirted all over the prisoners-workers. The SS man operating the excavator often dumped the corpses directly onto the prisoners working nearby, wounding them seriously.[52]

A more efficient method of dealing with the bodies of recently murdered prisoners was needed. In August 1942, work began at Auschwitz-Birkenau on crematoria equipped with large ovens and tall chimneys. The architectural plans were labeled "bath establishment for special action."[53] Eventually, five crematoria were built capable of incinerating sixteen thousand bodies a day.

The entire killing-cremation process as it eventually was developed in Auschwitz was a macabre model of efficiency. Victims descended a staircase into underground changing rooms adjacent to the gas chambers. Bodies were removed through doors on the far side of the chambers and, after "processing," were loaded on small carts. The carts were pushed along a system of rails to elevators, which lifted them to the oven rooms. Here, the bodies were systematically incinerated. According to plan, babies were used as kindling, with emaciated victims and then heavier bodies on top. Filip Müller remembered an SS sergeant's precise instructions as to his own favorite technique:

To get the stiffs [corpses] burnt by tomorrow morning is no problem. All you have to do is to see that every other load consists of two men and one woman from the transport, together with a *Mussulman* [an emaciated prisoner] and a child. For every other load use only good material from the transport, two men, one woman and a child. After every two loadings empty out the ashes to prevent the channels from getting blocked. . . . I hold you responsible for seeing to it that every twelve minutes the loads are stoked [shifted about with a poker], and don't forget to switch on the fans.[54]

Cremation Pits

The crematoria, however efficient their design and operation, could not keep up with the gas chambers, especially at Auschwitz-Birkenau in 1944 when the Jews of Hungary were brought in waves. The Germans had to resume burning bodies in pits, but the pits were much more refined than before. They were about 25 feet wide, 150 feet long, and 6 feet deep. Alternating layers of bodies and dry branches were stacked until the pyre stood about three feet above ground level. It took nine of these pits to handle the bodies of the Hungarian Jews.

After it was ignited, the fire was tended by *Sonderkommando* stokers. A narrow channel had been dug the length of the pits, with smaller channels sloping to the sides. Sizzling fat from the corpses flowed through the channels and was collected by workers using buckets on the ends of long poles. The fat was then poured over the pyre as additional fuel.

Crematory ovens still hold the charred remains of prisoners. Scenes such as these awaited the death camps' liberators.

The Disposal Problem

Killing the millions of people who came to the death camps was less difficult than disposing of their bodies. Camp officials found dealing with the sheer numbers of corpses and maintaining the secrecy impossible. In his autobiography, excerpted in *Foreign Policy, War, and Racial Extermination* by Jeremy Noakes and Geoffrey Pridham, Rudolf Höss, commandant of Auschwitz, outlines his problem:

> Already with the initial cremations in the open air, it became apparent that this could not be continued on a permanent basis. In bad weather or a strong wind the smell of burning spread over several kilometres and caused the whole population of the surrounding area to start talking about the burning of the Jews, despite the counter-propaganda on the part of the Party and the administrative agencies. Although all the members of the SS participating in the extermination programme received very strict instructions to keep silent about the whole procedure, later SS court proceedings showed that the participants did not in fact remain silent. Even severe punishments could not stop people from gossiping. Furthermore, the air defence authorities complained about the fire at night, which could be clearly seen from the air. However, we had to keep cremating at night in order not to have to halt the incoming transports. The timetabling of the individual actions [gassings] was firmly fixed by the Reich Transport Ministry in a time-table conference and had to be adhered to in order to avoid clogging up and disorganising the railway lines concerned—particularly for military reasons.

After liberation, a soldier and a French inspector examine a crematory oven and the tongs used to drag corpses to the ovens. Appalling as these methods were, the Germans were proud of their "inventions."

Müller, who worked in one of the pits, recalled the hellish scene:

The corpses in the pit looked as if they had been chained together. Tongues of a thousand tiny blue-red flames were licking at them. The fire grew fiercer and flames leapt higher and higher. Under the ever-increasing heat a few of the dead began to stir, writhing as though with some unbearable pain, arms and legs straining in slow motion, and even their bodies straightening up a little, hesitant and with difficulty, almost as if with their last strength they were trying to rebel against their doom. Eventually the fire became so fierce that the corpses were enveloped in flames. Blisters which had formed on their skin burst one by one. Almost every corpse was covered with black scorch marks and glistened as if it had been greased.[55]

Willenberg wrote about his reaction to his first sight of the crematory pits at Treblinka:

I stopped in my tracks, paralyzed with terror. The sizzling, half-burnt cadavers emitted grinding and crackling sounds.

Dwight D. Eisenhower (front row, third from left) and other U.S. officers examine this gruesome, and to most, unbelievably horrific scene. On these racks the Germans burned the corpses of thousands of Jews.

The flames, once having enveloped them, either dissipated into little jets of smoke or reignited into a blaze which forced firewood and corpses into a devil's embrace. Here and there I could make out the torsos of men, women, or little children. The smell of burning flesh reached my nose and prompted a flow of tears.[56]

Handling the Ashes

The fires burned for five to six hours, leaving a layer of white-hot ashes, its surface dotted with hundreds of skulls. When water was sprayed on the ashes to cool them, the pit and everyone near it was enveloped in an oily, rancid steam. When the ashes were cool enough, workers jumped into the pit to shovel them out. Many of the bodies had not burned completely. Here and there, workers found fingers, arms, legs, and parts of torsos, remains that were redeposited in a smaller pit for a second burning.

Ash from both ovens and pits was carried aloft by the wind and settled throughout the entire camp. Gisella Perl wrote that it was "hot under our bare feet like the sand of the beaches under the feet where free people were spending their vacation."[57] Truckloads of ash were dumped in nearby rivers or into pits and covered with earth. At Majdanek, where more than forty-five thousand cubic feet of ash were discovered when the camp was liberated, some had been used as fertilizer on the gardens of the SS.

Some of the ash was used for a more devious purpose. When non-Jewish German prisoners died or were killed, notes were written to their families saying they had died "in spite of the best medical care and treatment with medicines."[58] Accompanying the note was an urn. "Needless to say," wrote Müller, "they were never the remains of any particular person; the urn was simply filled with a handful of ashes of which there was always a plentiful supply."[59]

Such was the fate of millions during the three years the death camps were in operation. Men, women, and children; old and young; laborers and intellectuals alike, "the wealth and poverty of all Europe met."[60] Eight or nine hours later, only their ashes remained. Even so, they perhaps enjoyed a kinder fate than those who had not been chosen for death.

Arbeit Macht Frei: Work Brings Freedom

When new camp arrivals were motioned to the right rather than the left by the SS selection officer, they were spared—at least for the moment—from death. Instead of being condemned to die, however, they were sent to a living hell. There was life in these death factories, but it was a life of hunger, disease, brutal treatment, backbreaking toil, and constant fear. As one survivor wrote, "Dante's hell is incomparably ridiculous in comparison."[61]

New prisoners were first shaved head to foot and women's hair was cut off to be sent to Germany with that of their gassed comrades. If a woman was lucky, her hair was cut with electric clippers. Otherwise it was hacked off with scissors. The shaving was also painful. Petro Mirchuk wrote that "the same razor was used to shave one or two hundred people."[62] Filip Müller remembered "a soapless cold-water shave with razors so blunt that the hairs of one's beard were torn out rather than shaved off."[63]

Disinfection—genuine disinfection instead of a trip to the gas chambers—came next. Danuta Brzosko-Medryk described how

women prisoners, naked and ashamed in front of leering guards, were treated in Majdanek:

A prisoner in his striped uniform is standing by the side of barrels with some stinking sludge, a device for spraying liquid in his hand. We line up in front of him. The bloke in stripes fills the bottle with liquid and, a smirk all over his face, he sprays the bosom of the inmate closest to him. Taken by surprise

Newly arrived male prisoners at Buchenwald are washed and shaved as part of the humiliating farce perpetrated to convince them that the Germans were concerned for their health and welfare. The process was painful and degrading.

she backs suddenly and pushes us back. *Hande hoch* ["Hands high"]. The hands slowly go up revealing to us the fight going on within the woman. Her arm pits get sprayed too. She goes away slowly, her head lowered. Now the next one. Disgusting burning liquid sticks to my thighs and arms. I run away with disgust to the hot shower to wash off the dirt and the degradation.[64]

Prisoners' Clothing

The prisoners were next clothed. In most of the camps, the standard uniform consisted of pajama-like trousers and shirts or dresses of a blue-and-gray-striped material with matching caps and wooden clogs for shoes. When the camps were crowded, however, new arrivals were thrown bits and pieces of clothing that had been worn by prisoners long since gassed. Such rags were the tattered remnants of everything from ball gowns to army uniforms. Coarse, serge trousers might be topped with a velvet jacket. "We came dressed like men and we left in wet rags," wrote Salmen Gradowski. "In these clothes we look like criminals or like confirmed lunatics."[65]

Each person's clothes bore a triangular piece of colored cloth identifying his or her category. Common criminals, many of them German citizens, wore green triangles. Political prisoners were labeled in red, homosexuals in pink, Jehovah's Witnesses in violet, and "asocials" such as prostitutes in black. Jews were given two triangles forming a Star of David.

Prisoners stand for roll call. Two prisoners in the foreground are supporting a friend to keep him from fainting and either being executed on the spot or sent to the gas chamber. Roll call was another arduous and useless task the Nazis maintained to wear down their prisoners.

Prisoners were also assigned a number, tattooed usually on the left forearm but sometimes on the back or the chest. For some reason, the Germans set a limit on the numbers used. At Majdanek, when the number 20,000 was reached, the SS began using numbers of prisoners who had died. At Auschwitz, the limit was 200,000. Tattoos were hastily applied under nonsterile conditions and frequently became infected. Much more painful, however, was the degradation. "It is impossible to estimate the effect it had on morale," wrote Olga Lengyel. "A tattooed woman felt that her life was finished; she was no longer anything but a number."[66]

The new prisoners feared not only for themselves, but also for friends and relatives from whom they had been separated. Their questions about the latter were soon brutally answered. When Lengyel asked a veteran prisoner what had happened to her family, she was told, "I can assure you that neither your mother, your father, nor your children are in this world any more."[67] One Sobibor

A Day's Work

Those spared temporarily from the death camps' gas chambers were usually assigned to work teams, or *Kommandos*. For most, the work was exhausting physical labor. The Germans intended that as many prisoners as possible would literally be worked to death and then replaced by newcomers. Edward Dolecki, in this passage from Rajca and Wisniewska's *Majdanek*, tells about a typical day:

After the roll-call is over and no one missing, order is given to form work kommandos. . . . They had allotted the forty of us to one kommando. We had picked our own *vorarbeiter* [foreman], a barber from Hrubieszów, Józef Zienkiewicz, later on camp executioner. The S.S. takes us into a store-house and gives every two a hod [a type of carrier] for carrying earth, bricks and other heavy loads. Then he leads us to a pile of stones, which we are ordered to carry to another place, about a kilometer away. Loading the bricks and stones on [the hod] must be done with the greatest of speeds, and then you carry them, and return with the empty hod, running. After several turns we feel completely exhausted. The hod falls out of your hands, you have to gasp for breath. Even that is difficult to manage. Over you, there is an S.S. [man] standing with a horsewhip at the ready, and whoever wants to stretch his back gets a heavy blow. The *vorarbeiter*, armed with a spade handle, possibly is not willing to be any less active, and all the loiterers get mercilessly flogged by him. We nearly drop, dog-tired. Mouth dries up without water. The greatest desire now is for a drop of water, to ease the parched lips. Not allowed. . . . We nearly fail. Yet somehow you must stand it, maybe it will change, and if not, a day or two of such torture is enough to finish even the toughest person.

prisoner inquired about the pervasive smell of burning. "They are burning the bodies of your friends who arrived with you," [68] was the answer.

The newcomers received equally shocking information about their own fates. Samuel Willenberg was told, "Every one of us . . . is a corpse whose life has been prolonged a little. It's pure chance that we're still alive. Between ourselves and those who go to the gas chambers there's only one difference: they're gassed and we will be shot." [69] Such blunt pronouncements had a devastating effect on the prisoners. Many lost hope. Gradowski wrote, "Men do not come here to live but to die, sooner or later. There is no room for life here. It is the residence of death." [70]

The Barracks

The prisoners' actual residences—the barracks—certainly echoed Gradowski's gloom. They were built of one layer of planks, too thin and ill fitted to keep out wind and rain. There were no windows; the only light and ventilation came through open skylights at each end. The basic design was one used by the German army for stables. Indeed, some barracks at Auschwitz had formerly been stables and bore signs saying, "Mangy animals to be separated immediately." [71]

Three-tiered bunk beds made of rough boards lined each side. Three or four prisoners slept—often without mattresses or blankets—in a space designed for one. The

An Auschwitz barracks shows the conditions Jews endured. Prisoners were crammed into bunks where they slept the sleep of the exhausted.

beds were made even more miserable by the lice that infested the blankets and the prisoners' clothing. Prisoners scratched themselves until they bled. "Working with one's nails was not sufficient," wrote Alfred Kwiatkowski of Majdanek. "We shook them off our shirts onto the floor and trampled on them." [72]

The prisoners also shared their quarters with hordes of rats, which sometimes on the coldest nights would snuggle next to them for warmth. Often, when an inmate died during the night, the rats "would get at the body before it was cold, and eat the flesh in such a way that it was unrecognizable before morning."[73]

Living conditions were far better for the prisoners put in charge of their fellows by the Germans. The chief prisoner was called the *Lagerältester*, or camp elder, under whom served the block elders, barracks chiefs, and their various assistants. Each work *Kommando*, or team, was headed by a *Kapo*, from the Italian word for head. Most of the inmate officials were German citizens. Many were common criminals, picked by the SS for their brutality to rule over the other prisoners. They had private, heated rooms, personal servants, and food equal to that of the guards.

The ordinary inmate's diet, however, was both sparse and wretched. Breakfast was a cup of imitation coffee brewed from acorns. Lunch was a bowl of thin soup of varied ingredients: horsemeat, turnips, rotten potatoes, tufts of hair, an occasional

Prisoners with mess kits make their way to the camp kitchen at Dachau. Meals were often nothing more than a bit of thin soup and a piece of hard, moldy bread. On this meager food they were supposed to perform physical labor that would be demanding for well-fed individuals.

Night in the Death Camps

During the day, death camp prisoners were forced to work at a breakneck pace, always fearful of punishment should they pause for an instant. Only at night did they have time to themselves. Sometimes it was peaceful; sometimes not. Samuel Willenberg in *Surviving Treblinka* gives this description of night in the death camp barracks:

> We would welcome the night and the few hours of relative quiet that we had for sleeping. Sleep allowed us to forget the harsh life in the camp, dulled our suffering and sometimes transported us to a dreamland where everything was fantasy. But usually nightmares came to haunt us, actually they were the impressions of what we had seen during the day. Because we were suffering from sickness and weakness and from hunger and hard labor, into our sleep came all kinds of weird thoughts, extraordinary notions that, combined with the hallucinations that ruled our subconscious, expressed themselves in nightmares and horrible dreams. Sometimes the stillness of night was broken by a sigh or scream; sometimes by the muffled cough of someone suffering from tuberculosis, or someone snoring loudly. Here and there someone would wake up, let out a juicy curse, punch his noisy neighbor and then fall back to sleep—which was more of a snatched nap. But there were also nights with no sleep, full of work, beatings, and endless running.

After liberation the dead and dying lie in the straw on the floor of the concentration camp at Nordhausen.

dead mouse. In the evening inmates were served bread made mostly from sawdust. Prisoners were supposed to have a daily diet of 1,500 calories, even though 4,800 is required for heavy labor. In practice, they received far less.

The Fight for Food

Terrible as the food was, prisoners would go to any length to get it, including stealing it from their comrades. "The great writer who could describe the hunger we had to endure at Auschwitz has yet to be born,"[74] wrote Gisella Perl. She had to share a bowl with several other women, everyone watching greedily to see that no one got more than ten mouthfuls of soup before passing it on. They ignored the fact that their bowl had been taken by the barracks elder for use as a toilet the night before.

Prisoners ate and drank anything they could. In the heat of summer they died in agony after lapping up stagnant water from puddles. Mirchuk once found a hunk of spoiled, foul-smelling sausage in a garbage can. "After some deliberation," he wrote, "I decided that roses were for smelling and sausage was for eating."[75]

When prisoners entered Auschwitz, they passed through a gate under a sign devised by Höss, *Arbeit Macht Frei*—Work Brings Freedom. In reality, work more often brought death. The food was deliberately insufficient in both quality and quantity for the heavy labor most of the prisoners performed, all part of the Nazi scheme to work as many into the grave as possible. When there was not enough work to go around, inmates were made to do pointless tasks such as carrying heavy stones from one place to another and back again.

Most of the time, however, there was plenty of work to be done, much of it

This cynical slogan above the entrance to the death camp at Theresienstadt—"Work Brings Freedom"—greeted prisoners upon their arrival.

expanding the camps themselves. The prisoners were assigned to various *Kommandos;* there were teams for construction, road building, street cleaning, repairing clothing, cooking food, and all aspects of camp life. The Germans even formed a *Scheisskommando* to make sure no one stayed in the latrines longer than one minute. In a true example of SS humor, the *Scheisskommando* workers were dressed as Orthodox Jewish rabbis and large alarm clocks were hung about their necks in crude parody of prayer shawls.

The Germans seemed to take a perverse delight in assigning people to tasks for which they were unsuited. Illiterate laborers were given office work while intellectuals were used as porters. The most degrading work, cleaning latrines, was reserved for professors or rabbis.

Sorting the Spoils

The best jobs in the camps were sorting and storing the spoils of the victims of the gas chambers. So prized were these jobs that those who held them were called *Hofjuden*, or "court Jews." In Auschwitz, an area known as Canada (the prisoners imagined Canada as a land of immense wealth) contained warehouses stuffed with plunder awaiting shipment to Germany. Despite being watched closely and threatened with severe punishments, workers in Canada managed to pilfer items to trade for food and favors. Often, they used such items to bribe the guards to look the other way while they traded with one another.

Some of the most coveted duties in Sobibor were held by women who were given wool from the luggage of murdered Jews and made to knit socks and sweaters for the SS men. These women were housed by themselves in a spotless hut and given plenty of soap and water. The Germans did not want their own clothing ridden with lice.

Prisoners sort and transfer the personal belongings taken from newly arrived prisoners. These jobs were highly coveted because they spared the inmates hard physical labor, and they allowed them to steal items to trade for food and to bribe guards.

Not all jobs involved work at the camps. At Auschwitz and Majdanek, prisoners were marched to nearby factories. Thirty-four companies set up plants near Auschwitz to take advantage of slave labor and thereby made huge profits. Some, like I.G. Farben, Bayer, Siemens, Krupp, and AEG Telefunken, remain giants of industry today. The companies paid about a dollar a day per person, all of which went to the SS.

Certainly the most bizarre duties were those required of the musicians. Every camp had an orchestra, ranging in size and skill from three or four amateurs to a dozen or so talented professionals. The conductor of the Treblinka orchestra was Artur Gold, who had been one of the best-known conductors in Warsaw. Treblinka SS officers were so proud of their orchestra that they outfitted the musicians in white suits with blue lapels.

In bizarre juxtaposition, an orchestra made of prison inmates plays before a barracks as part of a celebration for returning troops.

The Auschwitz orchestra played each morning as the inmates went off to work. "It was like a very large group of skeletons marching to the sound of beautiful music," [76] wrote Mirchuck. The orchestras also played when transports arrived as part of the Germans' attempt to calm the new arrivals. At Treblinka, a group of musicians played near the gas chambers to drown out the screams from inside.

Gold even wrote a camp anthem for Treblinka:

We look straight out at the world,
The columns are marching off to their work.
All we have left is Treblinka,
It is our destiny.

We heed the commandant's voice,
Obeying his every nod and sign.
We march along together
To do what duty demands.

Work, obedience, and duty
Must be our whole existence.
Until we, too, will catch a glimpse at last
Of a modest bit of luck. [77]

The *Sonderkommando*

The worst jobs, both physically and mentally, were those of the *Sonderkommando*, the so-called special team that dealt with the

The *Sonderkommando*

Of all the work assignments in the death camps, those of the *Sonderkommando*, the "special team," were the worst. Not only was the labor physically demanding, but it also was mentally and psychologically draining. The *Sonderkommando* worked with the dead, hauling them from the gas chambers, cremating them, disposing of their ashes.

Filip Müller was one of very few survivors of the last Auschwitz-Birkenau *Sonderkommando*. In his book *Eyewitness Auschwitz*, he gave this account of the crematoria ovens at Birkenau and his work there:

> Five ovens, each with three combustion chambers, were installed here. Outwardly the fifteen arched openings did not significantly differ from those at the Auschwitz crematorium. The one important innovation consisted of two rollers, each with a diameter of 15 centimeters, fixed to the edge of each oven. This made it easier for the metal platform to be pushed inside the oven. The process of cremating corpses was similar to that in Auschwitz. The only way in which this death factory differed from the one in Auschwitz was its size. Its fifteen huge ovens, working non-stop, could cremate more than 3,000 corpses daily. Bearing in mind that scarcely more than 100 metres away there was another crematorium with the same capacity, and still another 400 metres further on the two smaller crematoria 4 and 5, with eight ovens each, one was forced to conclude that civilization had come to an end. And yet, whoever wanted to stay alive had to ignore the detestable reality and the conditions under which he was forced to live, however violently he loathed them.

extermination victims. The *Sonderkommando* lived close to the gas chambers, segregated from the other prisoners as part of the Germans' attempt to keep the mass murders secret. A camouflage *Kommando* built high fences to screen their area from the rest of the camp, but they could not prevent the truth from getting out. In Sobibor, a message was smuggled into the *Sonderkommando* camp asking what was taking place there. A reply came back: "Here the last human march takes place, from this place nobody returns. Here the people turn cold." [78]

Into the hands of the *Sonderkommando* came thousands of bodies, sometimes the bodies of friends and family members. Day after day, they dragged people from gas chambers, shoved them into ovens, shoveled their ashes out of pits. Some, after a while, lost all sense of themselves. Salmen Lewental wrote that his fellow workers "simply forgot what they were doing . . . and with time . . . they got so used to it that it was even strange to weep and complain." [79] Reality, however, had a way of piercing the numbness. Willenberg caught himself searching out the bodies of children to carry because they were lighter. "Here's what we've come to," he suddenly thought, "looking for children's corpses to make things easier for ourselves."[80]

The men of the *Sonderkommando* had no illusions as to what awaited them. "We had become privy to a great secret,"[81] wrote Filip Müller. At first, *Sonderkommando* workers themselves were frequently killed and replaced as part of the secrecy effort. As the volume of killings increased, however, a trained, efficient workforce was desirable and they were kept alive for months instead of weeks.

The isolated *Sonderkommando* was not forced to undergo one of the most bizarre rituals of the death camps—roll call. The SS fanatically accounted for every inmate each morning and evening. All prisoners had to be present; even those who had died during the night were laid on the ground as part of the formation. "Life is not important at the roll-call," wrote Gradowski. "Numbers are important."[82]

The Cap Drill

The SS also used roll calls as a form of punishment. Prisoners had to practice removing their caps and slapping them against their legs in unison. The sergeant in charge would yell, *"Mützen ab! Mützen auf!"* ("Caps off! Caps on!") over and over. Anyone late by a fraction of a second was clubbed by guards. By the time the sergeant was satisfied, the

A drawing made by a prisoner shows patients of the hospital at Auschwitz loaded onto wagons for transport to the gas chambers.

drill had gone on for hours and almost every face was covered with blood.

Roll calls were bad enough when the tally of prisoners was correct, "but the day of judgment descended upon us when they could not make up the actual number of prisoners."[83] The prisoners were kept in formation for hours, even in the worst weather, until a missing prisoner was accounted for.

The worst roll calls occurred after an escape. On one November day at Auschwitz-Birkenau, the entire camp had to stand at attention from early morning until nightfall. "From dawn heavy rain or sleet had been driving down and a strong northeast wind was blowing," a victim later recalled. "From noon onwards frozen men began to be carried or brought in [to the barracks] on barrows . . . half conscious, crawling, reeling like drunks, babbling incoherently and with difficulty, covered with spittle and foaming at the mouth, dying, gasping their last breath."[84] Another time, while the SS hunted down an escapee, prisoners were kept standing at attention for thirty-six hours, during which hundreds collapsed and died from weakness and exposure to harsh weather.

Roll calls also served as junctures for additional selections for the gas chambers. Prisoners took great pains to appear healthy. "Never, even in the best of times, did we shave so often as in Treblinka,"[85] wrote Abraham Kszepicki. Women pricked their fingers and rubbed blood on their cheeks to make them appear more rosy.

At all costs, prisoners wanted to avoid becoming a *Muselmann*, slang common to

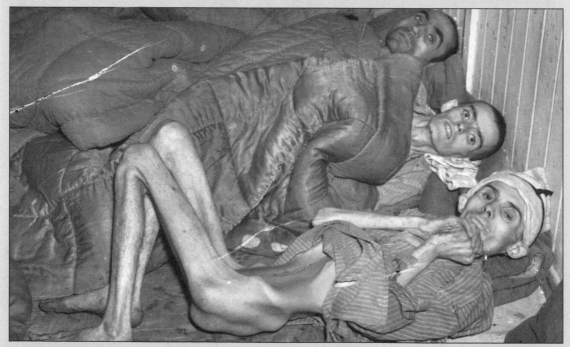

The results of Hitler's grand "Final Solution" after liberation at Buchenwald. For many, liberation had come too late to save them. The man in the foreground is so emaciated that his backbone can be seen from the front of his body.

all the death camps for someone who, irreversibly broken by work, disease, and starvation, was little more than a walking corpse. "The face looked like a mask with a faraway look in the eyes and the pupils unnaturally enlarged," a doctor testified at the trial of Rudolf Höss. "Such sick people saw and heard badly. Perception, thinking, and all reactions were slowed down."[86] The origin of the term is uncertain, but some have suggested that the *Muselmänner*, or "Muslims," got their name because they reminded other inmates of starving beggars in the Middle East, or because a bandaged head might be likened to a turban. "They had become nothing but skin and bones," wrote Müller. "Often their bones had rubbed through their thin parchment-like skins, resulting in inflamed and festering wounds."[87]

Killing the Sick

Illness was a virtual death sentence—death not from the illness itself, but from the SS, who weeded out those unable to work and killed them in the gas chambers or with a quick bullet. There were hospitals in the camps, primitive facilities in which inmate doctors did what they could with almost no medicine or instruments. Contagious cases were confined in a room called the *Durchgangszimmer*, or passageway, with nothing to eat until vans carted them off to extermination.

Pregnancy could also prove fatal. Some women were in the early stages of pregnancy when they arrived. Some managed to become pregnant in the camps despite the segregation of the sexes. They were in danger because as soon as a child was safely delivered, baby and mother were sent straight to the gas chambers. So, in order to save the mothers, inmate doctors killed their babies and told the Germans the infants had been born dead. "We pinched and closed the little tike's nostrils and when it opened its mouth to breathe, we gave it a dose of a lethal product," wrote Lengyel. "And so, the Germans succeeded in making murderers of even us. To this day the picture of those murdered babies haunts me."[88]

Such was the way of life and death in the camps. Those who made it through the initial selections at the train stations were beaten, starved, worked like slaves, and subjected to every form of degradation. That thousands died is not surprising. The wonder is that any survived at all.

Untermenschen:
The Subhumans

What took place in the minds of the death camp prisoners, even as their bodies suffered? They had been ordinary people leading ordinary lives. Suddenly, they had been thrust into an extraordinary situation, one in which few of the old rules seemed to apply. They had done nothing wrong. Why was this happening to them? Some lost hope, some preyed on their comrades, some became heroes, some lost their faith, some lost their minds.

Some prisoners simply could not, or would not, believe what was happening to them. They ignored what others told them and the evidence of their own eyes, ears, and noses. They could not comprehend anything as horrible as the Holocaust, though they were in its midst.

In 1943, Jews from the Czechoslovakian ghetto of Theresienstadt, which had been established to house the most prominent Jews from throughout Europe, were put in the "Family Camp" at Auschwitz. Men, women, and children were allowed to live together, wear civilian clothes, and perform only light work. When other prisoners tried to warn them they were to be exterminated and urged them to revolt, they refused to believe it. "The people in the Family Camp did not want to know about the peril in which they found themselves,"[89] wrote Filip

Müller. They argued that the Germans could have killed them long ago. They argued that—as the SS had told them—they were under the protection of the International Red Cross. A few days later, all five thousand Jews in the Family Camp were gassed.

Some inmates found life in the camps so awful that they jumped at any alternative. When Olga Lengyel was selected for execution with some other women, she told a friend they must escape. "No," replied her friend, "the camp is so terrible that no matter where they take us, it must be an improvement. I shall not escape."[90] Lengyel did escape and managed to survive until the end of the war.

Others knew their fate but accepted it without question. Many Jews, whose people had been persecuted for thousands of years, considered what befell them in the death camps part of God's ultimate plan for his Chosen People. A *Sonderkommando* worker facing execution told his fellows, "We must accept, resignedly, as sons of Israel should, that this is the way things must be. God has so ordained it. Why? It is not for us, miserable humans, to seek the answer. This is the fate that has befallen us."[91]

Suicide

While some accepted death, others longed for it. They had been torn from their families.

Salmen Gradowski wrote how those who had been left behind longed for an instant death "in which we might have reached the place of our beloved families and so would become united with them for ever."[92] A woman in Auschwitz wrote that after being shut up in a barracks three days and nights without food or water she wished only that she had been shot or gassed.

Many prisoners acted on their death wishes. Suicide was an everyday occurrence as people reached the limits of their endurance. Most who took their own lives did so at night. During the day, they had little time to dwell on their situation. After dark, in the misery of the barracks, thoughts of their former lives and their now-dead families proved too much to bear.

The most common method of suicide was hanging. Prisoners climbed to the top tier of bunks, fastened one end of a belt or rope around their necks and the other end to a rafter, and stepped off the bunk. Yechiel Reichmann relived the first morning he woke up in the *Sonderkommando* barracks at Treblinka:

> I awake with a headache. . . . I see opposite me a man hanging, one who had hanged himself. I point this out to my neighbor, and he points in another direction; there two more men are

These prisoners will not survive to enjoy their liberation in May 1945. After surviving the horrors of Nordhausen concentration camp, no doubt dreaming of freedom, they are too ill to survive it.

hanging. Here it is nothing new. He tells me that today less people than usual hanged themselves, and every morning they remove from the hut those who hanged themselves during the night. Here they don't bother with little things like that. I look at those hanging and am jealous of the peace they know now.[93]

On some mornings, as many as fifteen prisoners would be found hanging in a single barrack.

The suicides infuriated the Germans, who viewed them as a violation of their role as masters of life and death. To try to stop the hangings, a few prisoners were exempted from daytime work and assigned to patrol the barracks at night. The suicides lessened but did not stop. Sometimes, when a prisoner successfully hanged himself, the night watchman who was supposed to have prevented it was himself hanged.

"Embracing the Wire"

An indirect form of suicide was to run while on a work detail outside the camp, thus inviting a hail of bullets from the guards. Prisoners did not often do this because they were afraid that they might only be wounded and not killed immediately. A more certain method was to run against the electrified fence that surrounded some of the camps. In Auschwitz-Birkenau slang, this was called "embracing the wire." Olga Lengyel wrote:

The barbed wire was the very symbol of our captivity. But it also had the power to liberate. Each morning the workers found deformed bodies on the high tension wires. That was how many chose to put an end to their torments. A special detail detached the corpses with hooked sticks. The sight of the misshapen dead

filled us with mixed sentiments. We were sorry for them, for such deaths were really horrible; yet we envied them, too. They had found the courage to reject a life which no longer merited the name.[94]

Those death camp prisoners who remained alive despite the physical abuse and mental strain found ways to cope. Many simply tried to shut themselves off, to suspend human emotion, close off their minds to their surroundings, and concentrate solely on existing. Tovia Blatt, a survivor of Sobibor, wrote that when she asked a veteran inmate why he

This Soviet POW committed suicide by charging the electrified fence at Mauthausen concentration camp rather than endure slow death in the camp.

Trying to Stay Human

Death camp prisoners resorted to any means at hand to preserve some semblance of the lives they formerly had led. Women especially, many of whom had come from middle- and upper-class homes, were disgusted and repelled by the squalor in which they were forced to live.

In Auschwitz, most women were issued a chemise, or shirt, usually made of cotton, to be worn under a kind of sleeveless dress called a jumper. Since most of the chemise was hidden under the jumper, women would tear off tiny squares of their shirts to use as handkerchiefs, washrags, or even toilet paper. As the women tore off more and more pieces, the shirts grew shorter and shorter. Finally, all that was left were the shoulder straps and a narrow band across the chest.

The SS eventually found out what was happening. Gisella Perl, in *I Was a Doctor in Auschwitz*, tells what happened next:

One morning at *Zählappell* (roll call), we had to lift our skirts and hold them up while laughing S.S. men walked through the lines, whipping our naked bodies and selecting many among us to die in the flames as a punishment for having damaged "camp property."

Perl wrote about a fellow prisoner named Lily who one morning was surprised by an SS guard who jerked up her dress and discovered only straps. "You revolutionary swine," he yelled. "Where is your camp chemise." Lily was beaten until covered with blood. A few weeks later, she was sent to the gas chambers.

"Even today when I hold a handkerchief," Perl wrote, "I fondly stroke it and cherish it as the wondrous fulfillment of a deep and great desire."

---

never cried, he answered, "We remain indifferent, and we live like animals, for the present day."[95]

Though they lived in unnaturally close contact and were linked by a common bond of suffering, prisoners were usually slow to form close associations. Chances were that family and friends who had arrived at the death camps with them were dead. Perhaps other inmates with whom they had made friends had also fallen victim to disease, starvation, or the sudden whim of a guard. It was little wonder, then, that they shunned relationships with their fellows. It was better to remain detached, they thought, than to suffer additional grief. Rudolf Reder,

one of only two known survivors of Belzec, remembered the deliberate insulation of the self: "We were one mass. I knew a few names, very few. It was meaningless for me to know who a man was or what his name was. . . . No one was interested in the other. We went on with our horrible lives in a purely mechanical way."[96]

A Sense of Shame

The workers of the *Sonderkommando*, especially, tended to become withdrawn and isolated. Although they had no choice but to carry out their grisly duties if they wanted to live, they felt soiled, spiritually as well as bodily. Helping newcomers into the changing rooms, dragging them from the gas chambers, throwing them into the ovens—such actions were abominations that, in their minds, made them less than human and unfit for normal human contact. It made no difference that those with whom they lived and worked were doing the same thing. Salmen Lewental wrote:

> We became quite simply dishonoured. . . . Such thoughts crossed the minds of each of us. We were shamed of one another and we dared not look one another in the face. Our eyes swollen with pain, shame, tears and lamentations, each of us burrowed into a hole to avoid meeting another.[97]

Such feelings were to torment many death camp survivors long after World War II. They had so successfully retreated from emotional contact that human feeling was impossible to express. Scores survived the death camps only to later commit suicide.

Indifference was not always complete, however. Samuel Willenberg's father had survived with him in Treblinka for many months, but one day when Willenberg was working in a crematorium, he saw his father's body among the dead. A fellow worker, who had retained his religious faith, started to recite a Jewish prayer for the dead. Willenberg's feelings, which had succeeded in damming up, suddenly poured forth. "I had come to believe there were no human feelings left inside me," he wrote. "But while my team-mate recited the *Kaddish* [the Jewish prayer for the dead] my soul mourned in pain and grief. As the flames busily devoured the mortal remains of my father, the words of the traditional prayer gave me solace in this hour of sorrow."[98]

A Test of Faith

The death camps tested people's religious faith to the limit. Some prisoners found comfort that heaven awaited them after the living hell they were enduring. One young boy who had somehow escaped selection at Auschwitz-Birkenau said, "I am not afraid. Everything here is so terrible it can only be better up there."[99] Many Jews looked for God to rescue them as their Old Testament ancestors had been rescued. A rabbi in Treblinka told his fellow prisoners, "In every generation, my brothers, there were Pharaohs who wanted to exterminate us, but—praise be the Most Holy—he has always rescued us from their hands."[100]

In some cases, prisoners not only kept their faith alive, but were also able to hold limited religious services. Indeed, the Germans seemed curious to witness the ceremonies of the people they had vowed to exterminate. In Treblinka, Jews were allowed to get prayer shawls and books from the warehouse where the goods of their dead comrades were stored and to hold services. In October 1943, Jews in Sobibor were allowed to celebrate Yom Kippur, the Day of Atonement, although in their isolation they were not sure of the correct date.

Some people in the death camps became religious in response to their surroundings. Abraham Kszepicki wrote that in Treblinka, "Different people reacted in different ways. Young people who had not been religious before joined the young *Hassidim* [Orthodox Jews] and together with them said the *Kaddish*."[101]

As the months passed and the slaughter mounted, however, many Jews began to lose their faith. "Where is God?" they demanded. In Treblinka, when some of his fellow prisoners began saying the *Kaddish*, Yechiel Reichmann screamed at them,

To whom are you saying *Kaddish?!* Do you still believe?! In what do you believe and whom are you thanking?! You are thanking the Master of the Universe for His righteousness, Who took our brothers and sisters, our fathers and mothers—you are thanking Him?! No, no! It is not true that there is a God in Heaven. . . . If there were a God, He would not be able to look at this great tragedy, at this great injustice, as they murder newborn children innocent of any crime, as they murder people who wanted to live in honesty and benefit humanity, and you, the living witnesses to this great tragedy?! Whom are you thanking?![102]

"Where Is God?"

Others continued to believe in God, but thought that God had abandoned them. Elie Wiesel, on hearing someone begin the *Kaddish* in Auschwitz, "felt revolt rise up in me. Why should I bless His name? The Eternal, Lord of the Universe, the All-Powerful and Terrible, was silent. What had I to thank Him for?"[103] To believe in a God who was either unwilling or unable to stop the slaughter was a greater burden for men like Wiesel than to stop believing altogether. When Yom Kippur came, Wiesel refused to fast as prescribed. He wrote that "there was no longer any reason why I should fast. I no longer accepted God's silence. As I swallowed my bowl of soup, I saw in the gesture an act of rebellion and protest against Him. And I nibbled my crust of bread. In the depths of my heart, I felt a great void."[104]

Since so many Jews went directly to the gas chambers, Jews who were selected for work were actually a minority in the death camps. Most of the prisoners were Christian. They, especially priests and nuns, had

no easier time than did the Jews. Lengyel wrote about a Roman Catholic nun who was forced to stand, nude, while SS guards stomped on her rosary beads and performed obscene dances while wearing her habit. The nun kept her faith through all manner of torture and abuse. "The priests and nuns in the camp proved that they had real strength of character," Lengyel wrote. "Apart from the clerics, only the active members of the underground, or the militant communists, had that spirit."[105]

Try as they might, the Germans could not eliminate normal sexual desire among the prisoners. They tried putting a chemical, saltpeter, in the food, but food was not plentiful enough for it to be effective. In most cases, men and women were kept strictly apart, but many found ways to meet. The latrine in the women's camp became a meeting place for female prisoners and the workmen who entered their camp. Guards, especially the Ukrainians, were easily bribed to look the other way.

Many women traded sexual favors for food or clothing. It was the only way they could stay alive. Beauty had a different definition in the death camps. Women formerly thought overweight were considered desirable in Auschwitz, where thinness was no longer appealing. At first, Gisella Perl was shocked at the amount of prostitution that went on. "But later," she wrote, "when I saw that the pieces of bread thus earned saved lives, when I met a young girl whom a pair of shoes, earned in a week of prostitution, saved from being thrown into the crematory, I began to understand—and to forgive."[106]

Love in the Death Camps

Genuine love between men and women was not unknown. Samuel Willenberg wrote that it was not lust that drove men to seek

The Gypsies

The Gypsies posed a dilemma for Hitler and the Nazis. These nomadic tribes were descended from the same Indo-Germanic forebears as were the Germans and thus technically were also "Aryans." Their way of life, however—wandering from place to place, sometimes stealing from local farmers and townspeople—did not fit the Nazi picture of what a pure Aryan should be.

Professor Hans Gunther, an ardent Nazi and a proponent of racial supremacy theories, came up with the solution. The Gypsies, he wrote,

> have indeed retained some elements from their Nordic home, but they are descended from the lowest classes of the population in that region. In the course of their migrations, they absorbed the blood of the surrounding peoples and thus became an Oriental, West-Asiatic racial mixture with an addition of Indian, mid-Asiatic, and European strains. Their nomadic mode of living is a result of this mixture. The Gypsies will generally affect Europe as aliens.

Eventually, only a handful of Gypsies who according to the Nazis had maintained their racial purity were allowed to stay in Germany. On January 30, 1940, the rest were ordered into Polish ghettos, where they suffered the same fate as the Jews. In the Soviet Union, thousands of Gypsies were shot by the *Einsatzgruppen*.

On December 16, 1942, Heinrich Himmler ordered all Gypsies sent to the death camps. Sometimes, unlike the Jews, the Gypsies were permitted to live by themselves in family groups. They were not assigned hard work. Rather, they became traders, often acting as go-betweens for the Jewish and Polish prisoners and the SS. Prostitution was rampant inside the Gypsy camp, often with the knowledge and permission of husbands, brothers, and fathers.

Eventually, however, the Gypsies went to the gas chambers. Because they were a nomadic people not given to record-keeping, it is impossible to know how many were killed. Auschwitz-Birkenau alone claimed twenty thousand Gypsy lives.

out women so much as it was the desire to have someone to care for. Such relationships were usually possible only between prisoners who had some status. Jerzy Rajgrodski wrote about a marriage in Treblinka between a young woman and the prisoner-mechanic who was in charge of the engines that provided gas to the chambers. It was a traditional Jewish wedding, and even members of the SS came to the reception.

When ordinary prisoners fell in love, the outcome was seldom happy. A young man in Auschwitz, knowing he was to be selected for death, managed to use a stolen diamond to bribe his way into the women's camp where a secret marriage took place. When, a few days later, the young man was taken to Birkenau and the gas chambers, his bride's hair turned white overnight and she slowly starved to death.

Hate was perhaps a stronger emotion than love in the death camps. As they watched their families and friends murdered, many prisoners used hatred for the Germans to fuel the spark of life that burned within them. Willenberg once comforted a young man who had been selected for work but who was crying about the fate of his parents. "Relax Jezyk," he said. "No one cries in this camp; they just hate."[107]

Life in the camps was a day-to-day battle for survival, and the normal rules of right or wrong did not apply. "My every thought, every fibre of my being, was concentrated on only one thing," wrote Filip Müller; "to stay alive, one minute, one hour, one day, one week."[108] Sometimes the only way to stay alive was at the expense of other prisoners. In Auschwitz, the head of a *Kom-mando* killed his own brother when he fell and was unable to get up rather than let the Germans think he was soft. Some prisoners became informers for the Germans in hopes of getting a little extra food, but this was risky: If they were discovered, they were hanged in the middle of the night by their fellow prisoners and, when morning came, would be considered just another suicide.

Stealing was literally a way of life in the death camps. People simply could not live on the food they were given. They had to either steal food or steal goods to trade for food in order to live. Stealing, whether from the Germans or one another, was called "organizing" in Auschwitz slang. A kitchen worker might "organize" two sausages, one for himself and one to trade with someone in Canada for a new coat. Although prisoners

A group of Gypsy children comfort an ailing comrade in the Gypsy children's camp in Belzec. The Germans were confused about what to do with Gypsies, who originally descended from the Germanic tribes.

were not supposed to have cash, some of the money seized from those who had been gassed found its way into the camps' underground market system. Prices were high: $60 for a pound of margarine, $250 for a pound of meat. Even a single puff on a cigarette had a price.

Stealing to Live

The death camp system made thieves of everyone. Lengyel was once the proud owner

Dachau prisoners, perhaps recent arrivals as they appear to be in good health, stand in rigid formation as they await orders from their Nazi captors.

of a spoon with which she could eat her soup instead of lapping it out of the bowl like a dog. When the spoon was stolen, she found out that the thief was a woman who, before the war, had been a millionairess in Hungary. Women were afraid to leave their clothing while taking a rare bath for fear it would be stolen. "Women who had been mothers of honest families, who formerly would not have taken a hairpin, became utterly hardened thieves and never suffered the slightest feeling of remorse," wrote Lengyel. "Perhaps the Germans wanted to infect us with their own Nazi morals. In most cases, they succeeded."[109]

The death camps often brought out the worst in the prisoners, but they did not break the spirits of all the Jews. There were many instances of defiance. Even Pery Broad, of the SS, was impressed:

> The SS men had almost always the same spectacle before them—men and women, young and old, all those people managed to gather their last resources in order to die honourably. There was no abject pleading for mercy, often instead a last look of abysmal contempt, which made those primitive thugs [Broad's fellow SS] fly into a sadistic rage.[110]

In Sobibor, an old man on his way to the gas chamber recited the ancient prayer of the Jews, "Hear, O Israel, the Lord our God, the Lord is one." On the last word, he turned and slapped the face of an SS sergeant. He was yanked out of line and shot.

Over the Brink

Almost as difficult as holding on to one's life in the death camps was keeping a grasp on one's sanity. Beaten, starved, threatened day and night with death, prisoners often went insane. Samuel Willenberg, in *Surviving Treblinka*, gave this account:

> The harsh living conditions, starvation, over-exertion, and the constant pressure of fear occasionally drove someone insane. It hurt to witness someone go over the brink, and it hurt even more to see how the Germans mocked and abused the sufferer until they finally exterminated him in the *Lazarett*. I remember one night in particular. Most of the prisoners were sleeping, and a small group, wrapped in the traditional shawls, were praying by candlelight. Then the tranquillity of the night was pierced by insane laughter which sent chills down everyone's spines. The sound had something of the threatening cry of an owl, the sad cry of a jackal, and the crazy wail of the irrevocably condemned. The laughter occasionally broke off and the miserable soul uttered one word and one word only—"Mentsh"—Yiddish for "man." Then, without another moment's let-up, the insane laughter resumed. I had the feeling that I would be the next to act thus, that I would scream until my skull burst open and sent my brain spilling from it together with my torn, aching nerves. I buried my head in my blanket and plugged fingers into my ears to block out that deranged laughter. The doctors anaesthetized the man the next day and the "Reds" [*Sonderkommando* workers] hauled him on a stretcher to the *Lazarett*, where he was shot dead. Fortunately for him, he never knew what happened.

Bravery took many forms. Those who were about to die sometimes ignored their own fear in order to comfort others. A nurse in Auschwitz who contracted scarlet fever from her patients knew that she and her patients would be taken to the gas chambers as a routine measure to halt contagion. When her patients became afraid, the nurse calmed them, telling them they were all to be transferred to a larger, better-equipped hospital. "This young heroine," wrote Lengyel, "with her cool courage, had spared her unfortunate companions the usual torturing anxieties. What she herself experienced on her way to death one had best not even think of."[111]

The full range of emotions—hate, love, anger, courage, lust, envy—was present in the death camps. Emotions seemed to be magnified, however, by the pressure under which the prisoners lived. Generally, people behaved as they had before, only more so. The religious person's faith grew stronger. The person who tended to bully others became brutal. No one, however, could be in the death camps and remain unchanged.

CHAPTER 5

Übermenschen: The Master Race

The horrors inflicted on death camp prisoners—starvation, torture, brutality, degradation, murder—were, wrote historian Gerald Reitlinger, "inevitable things, given the nature of their masters."[112] What motivated the men and women who not only carried out such hideous crimes, but also often seemed to take pleasure from them? Some were ambitious. Some considered themselves professionals doing a thankless task as best they could. Some honestly thought their actions right and necessary. A few were compassionate. Many more were monsters in human form.

The Germans in the death camps were, as a group, unremarkable. Most were between the ages of thirty and forty, married, and came from lower-middle-class families. Before the war, they had been nurses, farmers, salesmen, factory workers. They had not been selected for their brutality. Indeed, few had criminal records. Some had enthusiastically joined the SS, but many had been drafted. And yet, these "ordinary" people were able, if not willing, to commit the vilest of acts against fellow human beings.

Part of the problem was that the Germans did not view the Jews as human beings, at least not on the same level as themselves. German hatred of Jews on religious grounds went back to the Middle Ages. More recent-

ly, Jews had come to be viewed by many in Germany as biologically inferior as well—as *Untermenschen,* or subhumans out to pollute pure German blood. Since the Nazis had taken power, the German people had been subjected to a steady stream of anti-Jewish propaganda. It was therefore normal for those who killed the Jews to think not in terms of murdering humans, but of exterminating a kind of vermin.

The war gave the Nazis the opportunity to turn their dream of a *judenrein,* or Jew-free, Europe into reality. In 1942, Hitler's minister of propaganda, Joseph Goebbels, wrote in his diary, "The procedure is a pretty barbaric one and not to be described here more definitely. . . . Fortunately, a whole series of possibilities presents itself for us in wartime that would be denied us in peacetime."[113] In wartime, previous stations in life meant little and societal roles frequently were reversed. A minor clerk who might have envied Jewish doctors and lawyers in prewar Germany was suddenly all-powerful when he donned a uniform. Jerzy Rawicz, in his foreword to a book on the SS, wrote that the death camp guards

were created by a criminal system thanks to which those who were of no account in society suddenly became masters over the life and death of thousands, hundreds of thousands, millions. . . . They reached the culminating points of their lives endowed with uncontrollable power.[114]

The Ukrainians

Only the officers and a few of the top enlisted men were members of the SS. The bulk of the guards were Ukrainians recruited after their section of the Soviet Union had been overrun by the German army in 1941. Most Ukrainians had hated the Communist government and welcomed the Germans as liberators. They were also even more fiercely anti-Semitic than the Germans, often gathering by the roadside to cheer as Jews were led to their death by the *Einsatzgruppen*. Willenberg wrote that "the dispassionate murder of Jews was their great joy in life."[115] One Ukrainian in particular stood out for his cruelty. Nicknamed Ivan the Terrible by the prisoners, he used a cavalry saber to stab the naked legs and buttocks of those he herded to the gas chambers and to cut off the noses and ears of others. Unlike the Germans, who took seriously the laws forbidding sexual conduct with Jews, the Ukrainians routinely raped Jewish women.

Many of the Germans, on the other hand, considered themselves above such brutality. They regarded themselves as professionals with a job to do. At his trial, Treblinka commandant Franz Stangl said, "That was my profession. I enjoyed it. It fulfilled me."[116] In Birkenau, Master Sergeant Gerhard Palitzsch was in charge of executing large numbers of people by shooting them in the back of the head. He took pride in his speed and accuracy. When he finished his deadly work, he would turn and stand stiffly at attention facing Colonel Rudolf Mildner. Mildner acknowledged his subordinate's expertise by smiling and raising his right arm in the Nazi salute.

A Nazi trooper proudly holds a Nazi flag aloft at a Nuremberg rally in 1933. Many Germans joined the Nazi Party and believed in Hitler's Final Solution.

Commandant Höss of Auschwitz-Birkenau felt the pressure of his job keenly—not because he was in charge of mass executions, but because of the demands placed on him from his superiors in Berlin. His complaints might have been those of a supervisor in any factory: quotas, deadlines, labor relations. He claimed he did not realize how many people were to be killed and that he was "helpless to intervene."[117] He claimed to have received conflicting orders—more deaths on one hand, more workers on the other. "The perpetual rush in which I lived . . . left me no time to think of anything except my work," he wrote. "I concentrated exclusively on this."[118]

Dedicated to Duty

Some of the SS took pride not only in how they did their job, but also in the job itself. Thoroughly steeped in anti-Semitism, they thought they were ridding Europe of a pestilence and making it safe for future generations of Germans. In a speech to the staff at Treblinka, an SS colonel told his audience, "Your work is a great work and a very

SS guards stand in formation at Belzec death camp. Many of the guards were given incentives if they were able to produce a large number of Jewish corpses.

A group of SS women await their fate after the liberation of Belsen death camp. The original caption of this photo claims, "all of the women are well-fed and show no remorse for their dreadful deeds."

useful and very necessary duty. . . . When one sees the bodies of the Jews, one understands the greatness of your work."[119] Some SS officers resented the fact that they had to hide what they were doing from the rest of the world. Odilo Globocnik, the man in overall charge of Belzec, Sobibor, and Treblinka, protested when Himmler ordered the bodies of Jews dug up and cremated in an attempt to erase evidence of their murders. "On the contrary," he said, "in my view bronze tablets ought to be buried, on which is recorded that we had the courage to carry out this great work which is so vital."[120]

Competition existed at every level of the death camps to kill the most Jews. Ambitious officers knew that promotions might be in store for those most effective in carrying out the Final Solution. Imfried Ebrel, first commandant of Treblinka, was determined to outdo his rival commanders. He had far more Jews shipped in than the camp could handle. As a result, piles of corpses lay unburied and rotting in the sun and mountains of valuable clothing were ruined. Ebrel was fired by Christian Wirth, who said that if Ebrel had not been a fellow German he would have been arrested.

Operation Reinhard

Reinhard Heydrich, chief of the SD, or security police arm of the SS, was the person given overall responsibility by Heinrich Himmler for the implementation of the Final Solution. It was Heydrich who organized and presided over the infamous Wannsee Conference in January 1942, at which plans for the extermination of European Jews were formalized.

Heydrich once served in the German navy but was court-martialed in 1931 because of his Nazi Party activities. He joined the SS the next year and quickly impressed Himmler. He played a major role in the 1934 "Blood Purge" in which Adolf Hitler had most of his enemies, both within and outside the Nazi Party, imprisoned or killed. He was made SS chief of Berlin and later, as chief of the SD, was the number-two man in the SS next to Himmler.

Heydrich was known for his ruthlessness. Assigned to Czechoslovakia to combat the anti-German underground, he had more than three hundred Czech resistance fighters executed in his first week there. On May 27, 1942, Czech patriots bombed and shot him while he was riding in his car on the Prague-Berlin highway. He died of his wounds June 4 in a Prague hospital.

The Germans retaliated by arresting and shooting more than a thousand Czechs suspected of anti-German activities. Lidice, the village closest to the site of the ambush, was wiped out. Women and children were shipped to concentration camps. The men and older boys, 176 of them, were lined up against a wall and shot.

In honor of his chief lieutenant, Himmler ordered that the extermination of the Jews in Poland at Belzec, Sobibor, and Treblinka be called Operation Reinhard.

Reinhard Heydrich, pictured in fencing attire. Heydrich was assassinated by Czech resistance fighters.

Enlisted personnel were also aware that they might be judged by how many people they killed. Ukrainian guards who shot prisoners trying to escape from work details outside the camp were given a day off. The more enterprising guards therefore told prisoners they would be shot if they did not start running and then shot runners in the back to claim their reward. In Auschwitz, large numbers of prisoners were supposed to be worked to death. When one block leader in Auschwitz reported a morning count of fifteen corpses, he was told, "That is too few."[121] The next morning, he reported thirty-five and was complimented.

The Germans' sense of duty and their view of the Jews as subhuman sometimes led to a remarkable lack of feeling. Some of them might as well have been dealing with sacks of grain as with living creatures. In fact, the murder of about forty-two thousand Jews in Polish labor camps in 1943 was given the code name *Erntfest*, or Harvest Festival. In Chelmno, where the gassing was done with exhaust fumes inside trucks, the SS worried about the "cargo" shifting. An SS doctor in Auschwitz-Birkenau was able to write in his diary about his excellent lunch of tomato soup, roast hen, potatoes, and ice cream followed in the evening by a "special action," one of the euphemisms for mass killing. And a brutal Auschwitz SS guard, shot in the stomach by a prisoner who had snatched his pistol, was able to scream out in his agony, "Oh, God, my God, what have I done that I must suffer so?"[122]

A Matter of Obedience

Other Germans, whether they personally hated, pitied, or felt nothing for the Jews, took the position that they were only carrying out orders. Höss wrote in his autobiography about a conversation with some of his staff:

Again and again . . . I was asked: is it necessary that we do all this? . . . And I, who in my innermost being had on countless occasions asked myself exactly this question, could only fob them off and attempt to console them by repeating that it was all done on Hitler's order. . . . There was no doubt in the mind of any of us that Hitler's order had to be obeyed regardless, and that it was the duty of the SS to carry it out.[123]

While many of Hoss's men disagreed with Himmler, "his person was inviolable [unquestionable]. His basic orders, issued in the name of the Führer [Hitler] were sacred."[124]

The Germans often attempted to justify their actions by claiming that the Jews and other victims of the Holocaust had brought destruction on themselves. Part of the Nazis' process of self-delusion was putting their victims in impossibly crowded, unhealthy conditions, starving them, dressing them in rags, and then pointing to their wretched state as evidence of their subhumanity. They established a system in which people were pitted against one another and in which only the strongest could survive and then accused the survivors of inhumanity to their comrades. Höss wrote that the Russian prisoners of war who survived Auschwitz "were no longer human beings. They had become animals who sought only food. . . . Those who had survived had done so only at the expense of their comrades."[125] He marveled that Jews could bear to work in the extermination and cremation areas, knowing that to refuse meant death: "The Jew's way of living and dying was a true riddle that I never managed to solve."[126]

Several Germans actually convinced themselves that they were acting humanely

An SS guard oversees prisoners as they are forced to dig a large trench. Many of the guards were pointlessly cruel and took delight in punishing inmates who were unable to maintain the swift pace of the brutal work regimen.

toward the Jews. Höss was relieved that victims would be gassed rather than shot. He congratulated himself that "we were to be spared all these bloodbaths and that the victims would be spared suffering until their last moments came." [127] Josef Mengele claimed to have saved thousands of lives as a selection officer, disregarding the fact that he condemned many thousands more to the gas chambers. Sergeant Robert Juhrs, who shot those prisoners at Belzec who were too weak to go to the gas chambers, said, "I regarded the killing of these people in this way as a mercy and redemption. . . . I shot these Jews with a machine gun, as they

stood on the edge of the pit. I aimed directly at their heads so that everyone died instantly. I am absolutely sure that nobody felt any torment." [128]

Wanton Cruelty

Despite German claims of professionalism, records left by death camp survivors are filled with accounts of pointless, deliberate cruelty. Such actions did not result in greater efficiency, but, as historian Daniel Jonah Goldhagen wrote, "had no instrumental purpose save Jewish suffering and German satisfaction." [129] The SS might have been made up mostly of "ordinary" people, but it had more than its share of sadists who have been compared to children who pull the wings off insects. According to Goldhagen, such people thrived in the death camps—"a world without restraint, a world in which the master could express in word and deed every barbaric desire."[130] Jews were tied to ropes and pulled behind trucks, the Germans laughing uproariously when they fell and were dragged across the rough ground.

All too typical was Sergeant-Major Otto Moll, the man who gave the order to drop Zyklon-B into the gas chambers at Birkenau. Moll delighted in making prisoners perform outlandish acts in the hope they would be spared. He once offered to let a man live if he could run barefoot across a pit of red-hot ashes and skulls. When the desperate man collapsed halfway across, Moll laughed and shot him in the head. Stanislaw Jankowski saw him order a young woman to sing and dance at the edge of a pit while he threw live children into the flames. When he finished with the children, he threw the woman in after them.

Another of Moll's favorite pastimes was to drag naked young women from the changing room and hustle them to the edge of a pit full of burning corpses for the sole

Instruments of Torture

Even the pleasure of music could be corrupted by the Germans in the death camps. Every camp had an orchestra of some kind; sometimes musicians serenaded the SS, sometimes they were placed next to the gas chambers and ordered to play as loudly as possible to mask the sound of screaming from within.

On one occasion in Belzec, the Germans postponed the murder of a prisoner in order to first inflict some mental anguish, using the camp orchestra to do so. This description of the scene by Rudolf Reder is found in *Belzec, Sobibor, Treblinka*, by Yitzhak Arad:

It was the middle of November. It was cold and all around was mud and snow. . . . The transport from Zamosc also included the *Judenrat* [Jewish council] from there. When everyone was already naked, the men were taken to the gas chambers, and the women to the hut to have their hair cut. The chairman of the *Judenrat* was ordered to remain in the square. . . . The SS men ordered the orchestra to the square. . . . I worked near there, so I saw the whole thing. The SS ordered the orchestra to play *"es geht alles vorüber, es geht alles vorbei"* ("Everything passes, everything goes by") and *"drei Lilien, kommt ein Reiter, bringt die Lilien"* ("Three lilies, a rider arrived and brought three lilies"). The orchestra was made up of a violinist, a flutist, and an accordionist. The playing lasted a long time. Afterward the SS men put the chairman of the *Judenrat* against the wall and hit him until he bled profusely. . . . Only at six in the evening did the SS man Schmidt take [the *Judenrat* chairman] to the pit and shoot him.

purpose of watching their reactions. "Just you look at that," he would shout into their ear. "Look at it well! In a moment you'll burn exactly like them down there!"[131]

While some Germans were curious about the Jews' religion and allowed them to conduct services, others took delight in mocking the faith of their victims. Sergeant Kurt Franz would single out Orthodox Jews arriving at Treblinka and ask them if they believed in God. If they said they did, he made them hold a bottle next to their heads. Aiming his rifle at the bottle, Franz would say, "If your God does, indeed, exist then I will hit the bottle, and if He does not exist then I will hit you."[132] Another example of SS humor was the ceremonial curtain from a synagogue placed across the entrance to one of the Treblinka gas chambers, the Star of David above the entrance, and a sign in Hebrew reading, "This is the Gateway to God. Righteous men will pass through."[133]

The "Medical Experiments"

The horror of the death camps is perhaps best illustrated by the bizarre "medical experiments" performed on some of the prisoners. Like so many others, these people suffered intensely, but their tormentors were doctors who were either sadistic or so unfeeling that they considered their subjects nothing more than laboratory animals—expendable animals, at that. In Auschwitz, chunks of flesh were cut from fresh corpses and used to grow bacteria in labs. An SS man said, "Horseflesh would do, but in war-time it is too valuable for that sort of thing."[134]

Some of the experiments were designed to support Nazi theories of racial superiority. Mengele was intrigued by the number of Soviet prisoners who looked more like the ideal German—blue eyes, blond hair—than most Germans. When he found suitable sub-jects from which to take skull measurements, he simply had them shot and their heads cut off. Mengele also tried to find ways to turn brown eyes blue by injecting them with various pigments. A visitor to his laboratory was aghast to see a collection of human eyes pinned to a board. "They were pinned up like butterflies," she said. "I thought I was dead and already living in hell."[135]

Mengele's greatest interest was twins. He thought that if he could discover what caused twin birth, he could use the knowledge to increase the birthrate of Germans. When transports arrived, he would walk quickly along the ranks of people waiting for the selection shouting, "Zwillinge aus!"—"Twins out!"[136]

Mengele's twins were first measured in minute detail, then subjected to various experiments. Some were deliberately infected with the same disease and then given different treatments to see which was more effective. On other occasions, twins' blood supplies were switched or they were given transfusions of different blood types. Mengele also forced twins to have sex with other twins to see if still more twins could be produced. Finally, pairs of twins were killed simultaneously so that their bodies could be dissected and examined for any anatomical differences.

Sterilization

Other experiments were designed to limit the birth of "inferior" races. Various methods of sterilization were studied to determine which were more effective and efficient. Clearly, the Nazis intended to sterilize large numbers of people in the conquered areas of Europe. Physician Viktor Brack once wrote Himmler that "castration by means of X-rays is not only relatively cheap, but also could be carried out on thousands in a very short time."[137]

A museum of Nazi barbarity. These items were seized by General George S. Patton from Buchenwald. Pictured are shrunken heads made from Jewish prisoners, parts of human organs, artwork sketched on human skin, and a lamp shade made of skin.

Chemicals were injected into ovaries and testicles. Victims were exposed to increasing doses of X rays so that the doctors could determine exactly how much would cause sterilization without causing death. At Auschwitz, an especially deceptive way of administering the radiation was to have victims stand at a counter and fill out a lengthy form, unaware that a hidden machine was bombarding them with X rays. When the doctors concluded an experiment, their victims were shot or gassed and sent to the crematoria. Filip Müller remembered bodies coming from the infamous Block 10 at Auschwitz as "horrible to look at. Often they had been dismembered or dissected. Many were the bodies of young men and women who bore strange burns and festering wounds on their testicles or the lower parts of their bodies, or abscesses on their bellies and thighs."[138]

Other experiments had to do with the ongoing war. In the interest of increasing the survival rate of German pilots shot down under extreme conditions, prisoners were made to sit naked in freezing weather to see how much cold the human body could endure. They were deprived of food

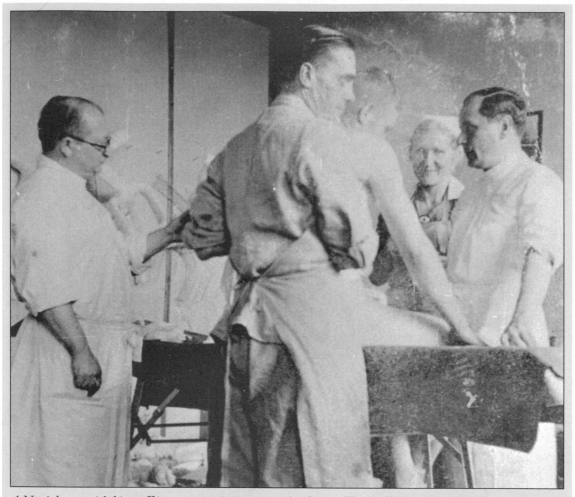

A Nazi doctor with his staff in an operating room at Auschwitz. The staff experimented to find a non-surgical method of sterilization for Jewish women.

and water to see how long they would live. The effects on the body of drinking salt-water were examined. Prisoners were shot or burned to simulate battlefield wounds so that methods of treatment could be tested.

Despite the fact that they produced few usable results, the medical experiments were considered very valuable by the Nazi leadership in Berlin. The SS doctors drew high, if roundabout, praise for their work. An evaluation of Mengele boasted that "he, as an anthropologist, has most zealously used his little off-time duty to educate himself further and, utilizing the scientific material at his disposal . . . has made a valuable contribution in his work to anthropological science."[139]

Acts of Kindness

While many members of the SS were undeniably cruel, a few went out of their way to be kind. Sergeant Herman Lambert, who headed a group of inmate builders in Treblinka, was horrified by the mass murders. "With regard to us, the workers," one man in Lambert's *Kommando* wrote, "he treated us very well. Frequently he would bring us food on the side from the German kitchen."[140] Sergeant Karl Ludwig not only brought prisoners in Treblinka extra food, but also even helped some escape. One labor camp commander near Auschwitz was well known for treating his inmates decently. When a prisoner asked him why he did so, since all prisoners would eventually be murdered, the commander answered, "I hope there will be enough among us to prevent that."[141]

Goldhagen's thesis in *Hitler's Willing Executioners* is that the Germans who took part in exterminations or exhibited extreme cruelty did so by choice, that they were eager, not forced, participants. SS troops had the option of seeking transfers from the death camps. There is no record of anyone in the SS being punished for refusing to take

A Prisoner's View of the SS

After the war, many Germans who served in the death camps claimed that they were only obeying orders when they participated in mass murder. Some maintained they were personally repulsed by what they were forced to do. Death camp survivors had a far different view. Samuel Willenberg, in *Surviving Treblinka*, told how the prisoners viewed their tormentors:

The SS men considered themselves an elite, ordained by the *Führer* [Hitler] for hard, responsible duties. This was a favourite topic of theirs in conversation with Galewski [another prisoner] who kept us informed on the intimacies of SS thinking. They spoke about the supremacy of the German race and people, their advanced culture and their important role in organizing and introducing the new order in Europe. Though they believed they were doing something natural and necessary, they were not carrying out others' will automatically. They actually took pleasure in cruelty, torture, the infliction of suffering. Their occasionally wild extremes in behavior presented their nature as an utterly incomprehensible riddle—human beings on the outside, and, as manifested by their actions, monstrous predatory beasts on the inside. How could one explain phenomena such as instructing prisoners who were condemned to death to organize choirs and orchestras, to dance, to play football, to box? . . . It was hard to picture these monsters as husbands and fathers who cared diligently for their families. Their bosses, though, cared for them well, appreciated their difficult position and rewarded them with frequent periods of leave in Germany. Every morning they did exercises, maintaining their health, and tried to keep the huts in handsome shape with flowerbeds and well-tended gardens, generally doing all they could to improve their living conditions.

A newly liberated Russian slave laborer points out a Nazi guard, claiming that the man brutally beat prisoners.

part in the Final Solution. After the war, a survivor testified at a trial about an SS officer who treated prisoners humanely. The judge, who had heard several defendants claim they dared not disobey orders, was amazed. "Do you wish to say," he asked the witness, "that everyone could decide for himself to be either good or evil in Auschwitz?"

"That is exactly what I wish to say," the witness replied.[142] As Goldhagen wrote, "The Germans could say 'no' to mass murder. They chose to say 'yes.'"[143]

Escape, Rebellion, Liberation

Many people picture the death camps as tightly sealed fortresses where people with no possible hope of escape went meekly to their deaths like so many sheep. Actually, escapes, while difficult, were by no means unknown, and both individual resistance and mass uprisings occurred. Especially late in the war, when Germans were hurriedly dismantling the camps in the face of the advancing Russians, the inmates realized that their only hope of survival might lie in rebellion.

Once people in the ghettos realized that selection for transport meant a journey to the death camps, some began trying to escape from the trains. The doors to the boxcars were locked tight, but some transportees who had brought tools succeeded in breaking through the wooden sides or prying up floorboards. Even if they survived the leap from the moving train they were usually shot by guards posted on the roofs. Those who did manage to escape and return to the ghettos were nicknamed "parachutists" by their fellow Jews. All too often, however, their escape was in vain when they were swept up for a subsequent transport.

Those who worked outside the camps had the best chance of escape. One man on a wood-gathering *Kommando* outside Treblinka was able to slip away when the Ukrainian guarding them got drunk and fell asleep. Belzec survivor Rudolf Reder had a similar experience:

> One morning I was told by the bully Irman that there was a need for tin in the camp. . . . I went with a truck, accompanied by four SS men and a guard to Lvov. After a whole day of loading the tin sheets, I remained in the car, under the guard of one of the bullies while all the rest went for entertainment. For hours I sat without moving. Then I saw that my guard had fallen asleep and was snoring. Without thinking, instinctively, I slid down the car. The bully continued sleeping. I stood on the sidewalk, appearing as if I were arranging the tin sheets, but slowly moving toward Legionow Street, where the traffic was quite heavy. I pulled my hat over my eyes; the streets were dark and nobody saw me. I remembered where a Polish woman, my landlady, lived. I went there, and she hid me.[144]

Hiding in Clothes

The best time to escape from inside the camp was during the confusion of arrival in the reception area. Workers sorting the

The huge piles of clothing and personal belongings taken from newly arrived prisoners were sorted and eventually redistributed to various agencies within the Reich. These frequent shipments allowed some prisoners to escape by hiding within or behind the cargo shipments.

belongings of those who had been sent to the gas chambers would build small caves called "bunkers" inside the giant piles of clothes. At night, after their comrades had been marched back to the barracks, they would emerge and climb over the fences to freedom. Simcha Laske, while loading clothes into a boxcar, found an opportunity to burrow under the pile. After the doors were closed, he "took a chance and stuck my head out of the pile so that I could breathe a little air. To my great surprise, I saw another head stick out from the piles of clothes. . . . Later we discovered another two boys in the car."[145]

In camps where the fences were not electrified, some prisoners managed to smuggle wire cutters into their barracks and to cut through the fences under cover of darkness. Other inmates tried to tunnel under the fences. On New Year's Eve 1942, five men in Treblinka crawled through a sixteen-foot tunnel prisoners had spent a month digging. Only one, however, was able to get away; the rest were caught. One was shot when he was captured, and the other three were returned to the camp and hanged in front of a special roll call. The last one to die, a man named Mechele from Warsaw, shouted as the noose tightened about his neck, "Down with Hitler! Long live the Jewish people."[146]

The punishment for attempting to escape was death, often a lingering, painful death. The Germans made examples of would-be escapees to deter other attempts. At Auschwitz, before being hanged, they were marched around the camp, signs around their necks proclaiming, "Hurrah, I'm back." In Treblinka, two boys were caught during an escape attempt. At the next roll call, survivor Oscar Strawczinski wrote, "The commander gave a short speech on the punishment of the escapees, and the two boys were hung naked by their feet. The Germans whipped their swinging bodies for about half an hour, until one of the Germans pulled a gun and shot them."[147]

"Collective Responsibility"

The Germans also tried to limit escape attempts through what they called "collective responsibility." That is, all the prisoners were held responsible for one another's actions, and when one succeeded in escaping, those who remained were punished. In Auschwitz, for example, there were twelve prisoners with mapmaking skills who worked independently of each other outside the camp, each with his own guard. When one succeeded in escaping, the other eleven were hanged though they barely knew the escaped man. When two men escaped from Sobibor, every tenth prisoner at the next morning's roll call was pulled aside and shot.

Despite such harshness, the Germans rarely succeeded in getting their prisoners to guard one another. More than 250 men knew about the tunnel in Treblinka, but no one said a word to the guards, even though they might have been rewarded with extra food. Workers whose comrades crept into clothing "bunkers" helped by piling up clothes across the entrance. The death camp prisoners knew that, since they all were targeted for death sooner or later, escape was their only chance, even though opportunities were rare and chances for success slim.

Prisoners resisted their captors in other ways besides escape. They often defeated every attempt to make them grovel before the Germans. One group of Hungarian Jews flatly refused to disembark at Birkenau, forcing the Germans to machine gun them inside the car. On another occasion, a Greek Jewess snatched a dagger from a guard, killing him and wounding another before she was shot down. Even after being crowded into the gas chamber at Birkenau, some Jews found the courage to sing the song "Hatikva," or "Hope," now the national anthem of Israel. A rabbi from France seized an SS officer by the lapels of his uniform and shouted, "You common, cruel murderers of mankind, do not think you will succeed in extinguishing our nation, the Jewish nation will live forever and will not disappear from the world's arena."[148]

Secret Diaries

Sometimes inmates chose to resist by trying to ensure that, even if they died, the story of the death camps did not die with them. Prisoners kept secret diaries and buried them in the hope they would someday be found. "Dear finder," wrote Salmen Gradowski, whose diary was found in 1945, "search everywhere, in every inch of soil. Tens of documents are buried under it, mine and those of other persons, which will throw light on everything that was happening here."[149] Even the workers in the cremation pits tried to leave evidence. Abraham Goldfarb wrote that "we secretly placed in the walls of the graves whole skeletons and we

The Punishment for Rebellion

Not all the victims of the death camps went meekly to their doom or submitted to German brutality. Sometimes, prisoners who could stand it no longer rebelled against the Germans or Ukrainians who were herding them toward the gas chambers or punishing them for some slight infraction. They could not have hoped to escape; instead, they felt a need, however futile, to lash out, to strike back.

Such occurrences drew harsh punishment, not only to the offending prisoner, but also to others who might have been innocent bystanders. Boris Weinberg, in *Belzec, Sobibor, Treblinka*, described the killing of SS master sergeant Max Bialas and the revenge exacted by the Germans:

At that moment a man jumped out of the ranks, ran toward the German Max Bialas with a drawn knife, and stabbed him in the back. He did the deed—then stood by, hesitating. One of the Ukrainians, Corporal Manchuck, saw what happened and ran over and hit the assailant on the head with a shovel he was holding. . . . With Bialas lying on the ground bleeding from his wound, the Ukrainians began hitting and shooting into the crowd. Dozens were killed and wounded. . . . Christian Wirth, who was still in Treblinka, was summoned. He ordered ten men to be selected and shot. Kurt Franz chose them, and they were shot in front of the roll call. . . . The next day there was no usual 6 A.M. roll call. The Jews locked in their barracks feared the worst. At 7:30 A.M. they were taken to roll call. It was held under a heavy guard of SS and Ukrainians. One hundred and fifty men were selected, taken to the ditches and shot as punishment for the killing of Max Bialas.

wrote on scraps of paper what the Germans were doing at Treblinka."[150]

On rare occasions there were major rebellions in the death camps. One of the first occurred on June 13, 1942, in Belzec. A group of Jewish workers, shocked and angered by the sight of bodies of women and children piled inside a gas chamber, attacked the guards, killing half a dozen. Most of the Jews were killed, but several escaped.

Two of the largest uprisings occurred within a few weeks of each other. On September 2, 1943, after months of planning and secretly gathering weapons, prisoners in Treblinka launched a rebellion. At 4:00 P.M. a member of the Treblinka underground, suspecting that an informer was about to reveal the plan to an SS sergeant, drew a pistol and shot the German. Although the killing started the revolt prematurely, prisoners were quick to react. Organizers began yelling "Revolution in Berlin!" as a signal to the others. Rifles were pulled from the grasp of guards and used against them. Hand grenades hidden in buckets of potatoes were thrown into buildings, setting several on fire. Two prisoners succeeded in blowing up the camp's gasoline storage tank, although they died in the attempt. Within minutes all Treblinka was chaos.

Hundreds of prisoners took advantage of the confusion to break through the fences and scatter in every direction. The original plan to destroy the guard towers had failed, so many fleeing inmates were shot down. Many more, however, broke clear. One was Yechiel Reichmann, who later wrote, "The murderers were chasing us with their machine-gun fire. Simultaneously a car was pursuing us, a machine-gun firing from its roof. Many of us fell. The dead were scattered everywhere. I ran to the left, while the car stayed on the road, firing. They were chasing us from every direction." [151]

Because of the premature start of the Treblinka revolt, few Germans and Ukrainians were killed or wounded. About 750 of the camp's 850 prisoners, however, were able to get beyond the fences. Almost half, 350 inmates, were shot by guards from the undamaged towers. Half of the rest were rounded up or killed within twenty-four hours, largely because the rebels had failed to cut telephone lines from the camp as planned. Of the remaining 200 or so, half

A photo taken of participants in the uprising at Treblinka. The uprising allowed a scant few prisoners—about one hundred—to escape.

were caught by German patrols or handed over by local peasants. The remainder, about 100 prisoners, were free.

The Sobibor Revolt

A few weeks later, on October 14, a similar revolt broke out in Sobibor. It was planned and led by a group of battle-hardened Soviet prisoners of war. The ringleader was Lieutenant Alexander Pechersky, a Jew from Minsk. Their plan was first to quietly eliminate the leading SS officers and sergeants and then take advantage of the disorganization of the Ukrainians to escape.

The greed of the Germans was to be their downfall. Shortly after 3:00 P.M., a prisoner approached SS sergeant Josef Wulf. A beautiful leather coat had come in a transport, Wulf was told, and it would fit him perfectly. Unsuspecting, Wulf stepped into the Camp I tailor shop. As the prisoner held out the coat, Boris Tsibulsky and an accomplice emerged from a hiding place and smashed Wulf's skull with axes. Next was Lieutenant Josef Niemann, who came to pick up a new uniform in Camp II. As it was handed to him, his skull was split from behind. Meanwhile, in the shoemaking shop, Sergeant Hans Goettinger was invited to try on a splendid pair of boots. He was killed as he was pulling them on.

The rebellion could not be kept secret much longer. According to plan, a Jewish prisoner blew the bugle for roll call. One of the organizers, Leon Feldhendler, arranged the Camp II prisoners in ranks and marched them toward the Camp I gate, singing a German song so as not to raise suspicion. An SS man saw them approaching and blew his whistle for them to stop. Pechersky later wrote, "'Hey, you sons-of-bitches,' [the guard] shouted. 'Didn't you hear the whistle? So why are you pushing like a bunch of cat-tle? Get in line, three in a row!' As though in response to a command, several hatchets suddenly appeared from under coats and came down on his head."[152]

The mass of prisoners then rushed the camp's main gate. Dozens broke through but were cut down by gunfire from the watchtowers. Another large group smashed through the fence and ran across a field that had been mined. The mines exploded, killing most of the first to cross them, but those who followed were able to get clear of the camp. In all, about three hundred prisoners escaped. Of these, two hundred managed to secure their freedom. It was the largest escape from one of the death camps.

Alexander Pechersky, the leader of the Sobibor uprising. The largest concentration camp escape attempt of the war, the uprising allowed two hundred prisoners to reach freedom.

The *Sonderkommando* Revolt

The final major death camp rebellion took place in Birkenau in October 1944. The gassing of the Jews of Hungary was winding down, and the *Sonderkommando* workers knew their turn would come soon. Their suspicions were borne out when a number of workers were selected for transfer to what the SS said was a work camp. Shortly thereafter, for the first time in the camp's history, the *Sonderkommando* was confined to barracks while the SS and Ukrainians handled the burning of corpses. They failed to do the job completely, however, and when the prisoners went back to work they were able to identify the charred remains of their comrades.

On October 7, the workers were lined up for yet another selection. When the SS sergeant in charge began to call numbers, no one stepped forward. The sergeant hesitated, then dispatched some guards to hunt down the men he thought were hiding in the crematorium. As the guards prepared to leave they were suddenly hit with a hail of stones thrown by the prisoners, who then rushed them. Some of the wounded guards were torn apart by the prisoners, but others were able to fire briefly into the crowd and then flee for help.

The uprising had not been well planned, and prisoners milled about in confusion. Some managed to set Crematorium IV on fire, and the sky was soon filled with smoke and flames. When SS reinforcements arrived, they poured machine-gun fire into the compound. The prisoners began to fall. Some produced hand grenades and threw them at the SS, killing several. Finally, those who remained rushed the gate. A few broke through, but most were gunned down.

Filip Müller, unable to reach the gate, scrambled for a place to hide. He ran into the burning crematorium and spotted one of the ovens. He crawled in and shut the door behind him. When he heard the shooting die down, he made his way to the chimney, where he had room to stand. He later described his refuge:

> As I glanced up I glimpsed, framed by the four soot-blackened chimney walls, a small square of deep blue sky. Still trembling with agitation I lit a cigarette and blew the smoke up into the huge chimney. As it drifted up I suddenly remembered the very many human beings whose mortal remains had gone the same way.[153]

Müller emerged from hiding about midnight and was able to blend in with a group who had been gathered to haul away the bodies of the slain prisoners. He was one of the few survivors. More than 450 prisoners were killed, either in the compound or in the surrounding countryside. Four SS sergeants and a dozen enlisted men were killed, the highest German death toll of any of the uprisings.

The Hostility of the Poles

One of the greatest difficulties facing Jews who managed to escape from the death camps was survival on the outside. Polish peasants nearby not only were fearful of punishment if they helped escaped prisoners, but they also tended to be anti-Semitic. The prevailing attitude of Poles toward the Jews was summed up by an article in a Warsaw underground newspaper:

> Within a short period, Warsaw will say good-bye to the last Jew. If it would be possible to conduct a funeral, the reaction would be interesting. Would sorrow or tears accompany the coffins, or perhaps joy? . . . Let us not strive for an artificial sorrow for the dying nation that was not close to our hearts.[154]

Most Poles simply refused all pleas for help, whether for food or shelter. Others actively joined in the search for runaway prisoners, hoping to collect a reward for their capture and return. Especially dangerous were the local people who pretended to be willing to help the Jews in order to extort money from them. Abraham Goldfarb, who escaped from Treblinka,

> met a farmer in the forest and asked him for some food. He told me to gather some mushrooms and that he would get me some bread. After a short time, he returned with another farmer. They grabbed me, bound my hands, and demanded money and gold. They took out knives and threatened me that if I did not tell them where I had hidden the money they would stab me.[155]

Not all Poles were hard-hearted toward the Jews. Rudolf Reder was hidden by his former landlady. And though Dov Freiberg, a Sobibor escapee, wrote, "More than once we considered suicide, after we saw that the whole world was against us," he added, "there were also a few good Poles and Ukrainians. These people helped us and risked their lives because they had to fear every neighbor, every passerby, every child, who might inform on them."[156]

The Poles were not the only people who seemed either indifferent or downright hostile to the fate of Europe's Jews. When news of the death camps reached beyond the borders of Poland, most of the leaders of the nations fighting Germany refused to believe it. Then, forced to believe it by the strength of the evidence, they seemed not to care.

Refusal to Believe

Even if they did not care about the Jews, the Polish underground had a vital interest in the death camps since the majority of the inmates were Poles and the camps were in occupied Poland. As early as March 1942, the underground funneled information on the camps to Poland's government-in-exile in London, which passed it to the British government and the British Broadcasting Corporation (BBC). The BBC refused to air the reports. A Polish official later told a member of the underground, "Your radiograms were not believed. The [Polish] government did not believe them, and the British did not believe them. It was said that you exaggerated your anti-Nazi propaganda."[157]

The story was much the same in the United States. Eyewitness accounts and even photographs of Auschwitz-Birkenau were delivered to the U.S. State Department. Officials there, some of whom were known to be anti-Semitic, claimed the evidence had been faked in order to inflame public opinion against Germany. Even those who were not anti-Jewish doubted the evidence. The entire concept of the extermination camps was too monstrous. As historian Otto Friedrich wrote, "What was happening at Auschwitz could not be imagined, therefore could not be believed, even when photographed, even when reported in detail by escaping prisoners, could not be believed and therefore could not be stopped."[158]

Inside the camps, prisoners dreamed of rescue. Fania Fénelon wrote that in Auschwitz, after a courageous Polish couple escaped together, "We could already see Mala and Edek returning at the head of millions of soldiers, who would enter the camp and put out the SS men's eyes, bayonet them in the stomach. We were drunk with images of gory revenge."[159] Those images were shattered when the pair was captured, returned to Auschwitz, and killed—even though both died bravely and defiantly. Olga Lengyel and her fellow Auschwitz inmates dreamed of looking up one day to see the sky filled with British and American paratroopers. "We would greet our liberators with kisses," she wrote. "It had not occurred to us that we were dirty and ragged, and our kisses would certainly be far from desirable. In any case, we decided that we would make beautiful dresses from the parachute silk."[160]

For the vast majority of death camp prisoners, dreams of rescue remained just that. Even when the evidence could no longer be ignored, military authorities refused to attempt to stop the killing. In vain, the World Jewish Congress and the Polish government-in-exile pleaded with the Allies to either bomb the gas chambers and crematoria or at least bomb the railroad tracks leading to the camps. The Allies refused. In answer to one request, John J. McCoy of the U.S. War Department wrote that such bombing

could be executed only by the diversion of considerable air support essential to the success of our forces now engaged in decisive operations and would in any case be of such doubtful efficacy [effectiveness] that it would not amount to a practical project.[161]

In spite of being hardened by scenes of war, these soldiers are visibly shocked by the useless slaughter presented before them. Stacked up like a macabre cord of wood and denied their dignity even in death, these men are a testament to the barbarities perpetrated against the Jews of Europe by the Nazi regime.

How Many Died?

One of the most troubling aspects of the Holocaust is that no one knows—even to the nearest million—exactly how many people were killed. Torn from their homes, packed into ghettos, carted to death camps, gassed and shot by the thousands, most of the Jews of Europe perished, as did uncounted Gypsies, Russians, and Poles. All too often their identities died with them as their identification papers and other documents were fed to the flames.

Russian figures put the total number of Holocaust victims at about 11 million, 4 million in Auschwitz alone. Rudolf Höss wrote that 3 million died at Auschwitz. However, most historians have concluded these figures are far too high, and at his trial Höss himself lowered the number to 1,135,000. Gerald Reitlinger, in *The Final Solution*, gives a total of 851,200 Jews as having been sent to Auschwitz.

The confusion extends to the totals for the other death camps. Estimates for Majdanek range from 74,000 to 200,000 to 370,000. Totals for Treblinka vary from 700,000 to 1.2 million. Only for Chelmno do the various estimates tend to agree—about 155,000 deaths.

The man in the best position to know the awful extent of the toll taken by the Final Solution was one of its prime architects, Adolf Eichmann. After the war Eichmann's colleague William Hoettl testified that in August 1944 Eichmann said he had prepared a report for Heinrich Himmler on the number of Jews killed. Hoettl said that "on the basis of the information [Eichmann] had at his disposal . . . around four million Jews had been killed in the various extermination camps, while two million had died by other means, of whom the majority had been shot by the *Einsatzkommandos* . . . during the campaign against Russia."

The figure of 6 million is the one generally accepted by most scholars, but all agree that it is, at best, an estimate and that the true extent of the Final Solution will never be known.

Only part of the gruesome story of Lublin death camp is told by this vast pile of shoes once worn by the thousands of men, women, and children who were herded through the doors of the camp.

The End Comes Slowly

Thus it was that the death camps came to an end slowly and more often according to a German rather than Allied timetable. By March 1943 most of the Jews of Poland had been exterminated. Himmler decided that Auschwitz-Birkenau could handle the flow of Jews from western and southern Europe and thus ordered Belzec, Sobibor, and Treblinka closed. Chelmno and Majdanek, which were not under Himmler's direct control, continued to operate along with Auschwitz-Birkenau.

The first of the camps to be closed was Belzec. In July, the remaining prisoners were shipped to Sobibor, and the SS sought to erase all evidence Belzec had existed. The buildings were dismantled and the cremated remains of the last victims were covered with earth. Grass and pine trees were planted atop the smoothed-out mass graves. The Germans, however, had not reckoned with the greed of the neighboring Poles. No sooner had the Germans left, according to a Polish farmer that lived nearby, than the area was "plucked to pieces by the neighboring population, who were searching for gold and valuables. That's why the whole surface of the camp was covered with human bones, hair, ashes from cremated corpses, dentures, pots and other objects."[162]

To stop the plundering, the Germans sent guards back to Belzec to chase the local peasants away. Globocnik then hit on a more permanent solution. Atop the graves, a farm was laid out and a house was built for a Ukrainian guard and his family; similar window dressing disguised both Sobibor and Treblinka. "For reasons of surveillance, in each camp a small farm was created which is occupied by a guard," Globocnik wrote to Himmler. "An income must be regularly paid to him so that he can maintain the small farm."[163]

Treblinka was abandoned in November 1943. Thirty Jewish prisoners had been kept behind to finish dismantling the camp. When they were done, they were shot in groups of five, each group being forced to cremate the bodies of the group before, with the last group being burned by the guards. Sobibor was closed the next month. The last of the prisoners were forced to lie down next to the cremation grills, where they were shot by the SS.

The Liberation of Majdanek

The Germans did not have a chance to shut down Majdanek in such orderly fashion. With the Russian army advancing westward, the evacuation of the camp began in March 1944. Although about fifteen thousand prisoners were shipped to camps inside Germany, another thousand—mostly those too ill to walk—remained when the Russians overran the camp on July 23.

With the liberation of Majdanek, the Allies were finally able to see for themselves the horror of the death camps. The Russians wasted no time in inviting representatives from the International Red Cross and the news media to view the gas chambers, the crematoria, and the survivors who were little more than skeletons. Even then, however, the governments of the United States and Great Britain hesitated to believe what had happened. Once more, officials dismissed stories and photographs coming from Poland as Russian propaganda.

The Germans, however, did not want a repeat of Majdanek. Later in July, the final victims at Chelmno were driven to their deaths in the special vans. The last remaining prisoners were shipped to the last remaining death camp—Auschwitz-Birkenau.

Throughout the last half of 1944, the Germans worked furiously to complete

Survivors stare out from the barbed wire during the liberation of Majdanek. As Allied troops entered Poland, Germans rushed to annihilate as many Jews as they could.

their deadly work in preparation for the evacuation of Auschwitz. In December 1944, a month after the uprising of the *Sonderkommando*, the Birkenau gas chambers claimed their last victims. Workers began taking apart the crematoria, although some of the ovens were kept in use for the burning of records. Trainloads of prisoners were shipped to Germany. When there were no trains available, prisoners were forced to set out through the snow on foot, accompanied by guards. Olga Lengyel was in one such group. "Then the SS closed the gates," she wrote. "Was it possible? We were leaving Birkenau still alive! After we

had traveled some distance, we came to a turn in the road. Here we looked back for our last glimpse of Birkenau where we had suffered such unbelievable trials."[164] Still more trials were to come. Thousands more would die on what came to be called these "death marches."

The Last Executions

On January 6, 1945, four young Jewish women who had smuggled weapons to the *Sonderkommando* were hanged at Auschwitz. As the noose was put around her neck, one of the victims told the SS guard, "I shall die now, but your turn will come soon."[165]

These were the last official German executions at the camp.

On January 17, the final roll call was conducted with Russian artillery booming in the distance. Shortly after midnight on January 18, the Germans dynamited the last of the crematoria and gathered all the remaining prisoners who could walk for the final evacuation. At about 1:00 A.M., the gates were closed, the electricity was turned off, and Auschwitz sank into darkness.

The prisoners who had been left behind survived as best they could. Primo Levi, who had been hospitalized with scarlet fever, remembered that all the "ragged, decrepit, skeleton-like patients at all able to move dragged themselves everywhere on the frozen soil, like an invasion of worms. They had ransacked all the empty huts in search of food and wood."[166]

On the afternoon of January 27, ten days after the Germans left, Soviet soldiers, dressed in white camouflage garb, emerged from the snowy forests. Before their astounded eyes were rows of barracks, miles of barbed wire. Fearing an ambush, they moved warily inside the gates. Instead of enemy troops, however, they found more

Allied soldiers march past hundreds of corpses after liberation. Many prisoners were being killed even while they could hear the artillery barrages of their approaching saviors.

The Death Marches

The closing of the death camps meant liberation for only a few of the prisoners, generally those who were too sick or weak for the Germans to take with them as they scrambled out of the path of the advancing Soviet troops. Some of the rest were "lucky" enough to be shipped westward in boxcars. The remainder had to go on foot through the frigid Polish winter. Their treks came to be known as the "death marches."

Petro Mirchuk recalled his own march from Auschwitz in his book *In the German Mills of Death:*

> After a few hours of walking . . . the first prisoners began to fall. Then we discovered an especially cruel procedure. As a prisoner fell, he was shot in the head and pushed aside. At the end of the column there was a group of ten SS guards who checked all fallen prisoners to make sure they were dead. They crushed the skulls to be sure that no one survived. We did not first understand the reason for this, but it

soon became obvious that we would be followed by the advancing Russians, and the Germans didn't want any living witnesses to their cruelty.

Still more horror awaited those who completed the death marches. Gisella Perl was in a group marched from Auschwitz to the concentration camp at Bergen-Belsen (sometimes given in reverse order) in Germany. She gave this description in *I Was a Doctor in Auschwitz:*

> Belsen-Bergen . . . was [the] supreme fulfillment of German sadism and brutality. Belsen-Bergen can never be described. . . . One must have seen those mountains of rotting corpses mixed with filth . . . where once in a while one noticed a slight movement caused by rats or by the death convulsion of a victim who had been thrown there alive. . . . There was no roll call here, no selection, no work, no order. There was only death.

Like these men from Dachau, many prisoners were force-marched to new locations just before the arrival of the Allied forces. The Nazis did not intend to leave any living witnesses who could bear witness to their slaughter of millions of human beings.

than seven thousand people, most barely alive. Those who could still walk converged on their liberators. "There was a mad rush to shake them by the hand," survivor Karel Ornstein wrote. "Several prisoners waved red scarves. The shouts of joy [could] have gone on forever."[167]

Although the Holocaust would claim many more victims in other facilities before the war ended a few months later, the murderous work of the six death camps was done. Three years had passed since the first gas vans had gone into operation at Chelmno. Millions of innocent people had been shot, gassed, and starved to death. It remained for those who survived, those who had liberated them, those who had taken part in the murders, and the members of future generations to search for answers to how and why such a crime could have taken place.

"There Is No Why"

Almost as tormenting as the brutality the death camp victims suffered was their bewilderment as to why it all was taking place. Why, they asked themselves and their captors, are innocent women and children killed? Why, when labor is needed so badly for the war effort, are millions of potential workers squandered? Why, when slaves are used, are they treated with unnecessary and wasteful harshness? Once, when Auschwitz prisoner Primo Levi tried to quench his thirst by sucking on an icicle, it was quickly snatched away by a guard. When Levi asked him why, the guard replied, "Here, there is no why."[168]

Sociologists, theologians, and historians have asked the same questions ever since the death camps were exposed to a horrified world at the end of World War II. They have had little more luck than Levi in finding the answers, but not for lack of trying. Hundreds of books have been written trying to account for the Holocaust. Theories are advanced; suggestions made; explanations offered. Perhaps the reason scholars are still trying to find the answer to the "why" of the death camps is that there is no answer.

Historian Yehuda Bauer lists eight factors in German history that contributed to the Holocaust, among them the German tradition of obedience to authority, the long history of anti-Semitism in Germany, the humiliation brought about by Germany's defeat in World War I, and the economic hardship caused by the Great Depression of the early 1930s. All were factors in the rise of the Nazis, but, as Bauer admits, "only some possible conclusions might be formulated as to 'why.'"[169]

Most of the victims had committed no crime, at least not in the normal sense of the word. Their only "crime" was to have been born Jewish, and as historian Ronnie Landau wrote, "their 'punishment' was—and remains to this day—inexplicable."[170]

The death camps cannot be explained in terms of ordinary human values. The foundations on which society is built—decency, respect for others, a sense of fairness, the rule of law—simply did not exist there. When the trains rolled through the gates of Treblinka or Majdanek, they might as well have been landing on another planet, not in what was considered an advanced, civilized country.

The Nazi Rationale

The Nazis, however, did not see the death camps in ordinary human terms. What they did destroyed—in their minds—not people but some lesser form of life. Jews, the Germans had been told by their leaders, by their philosophers, and even by their ministers,

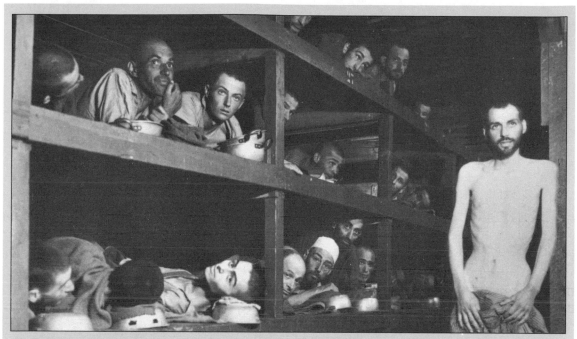

These death camp survivors will escape death at the hands of the Nazis, but many will be plagued by lingering illness and nightmares throughout their lives. The Holocaust did not end with the defeat of Germany—it continues to take its toll on the broken bodies and tortured minds of many who survived.

were subhumans. Not only were they sub-human, but they supposedly sought to reduce the Germans to their level by conta-minating their pure, "Aryan" blood. For Germans who believed this, there was no choice. One former *Einsatzgruppen* officer wrote, "What else could we have done when confronted with demons at work, engaged in a struggle against us."[171]

The most frightening aspect of the death camps, then, was not to be found in sadists like Otto Moll. Unfortunately, people who take pleasure in inflicting pain exist at any time, in any country. The true horror of the death camps and, indeed, of the entire Holocaust was expressed in the person of an SS man who told a fellow Ger-man to stop lifting little children up by the hair and shooting them through the head. "What I meant," he said later, "was he should not lift the children up by the hair, he should kill them in a more decent way."[172]

When any human being, much less hun-dreds of thousands, can reason in such a way, one must ask why even if there is no ready answer. It is temptingly comfortable to dismiss the death camps as the ultimate expression of a freak of history, a chance convergence of events that could not hap-pen again. To do so would be to ignore the fact that it has happened again, perhaps not on the same scale, but all too often. The underlying factor—an unreasoning hatred of one people for another—is still present. This being the case, wrote Bauer, "Who might the Jews be next time?"[173]

The Fate of Selected Death Camp Figures

Bouhler, Philip: Head of the euthanasia program in Germany and one of its founders. Believed to have committed suicide in May 1945.

Broad, Pery: SS sergeant in Auschwitz. Briefly imprisoned by British and then released. Arrested by German government in 1959, tried in 1965, and sentenced to four years in prison. Released in 1969.

Demjanjuk, John: Extradited from Cleveland, Ohio, to Israel in 1986, accused of being Ivan the Terrible from Treblinka. He was convicted, but the conviction was later overturned by the Israeli Supreme Court. Demjanjuk returned to Cleveland, where he still lived in 1997.

Eichmann, Adolf: Head of the Jewish section of the Gestapo from 1940 to 1945. Kidnapped by Israeli agents from Argentina in 1960, tried in Jerusalem, executed on May 31, 1962.

Frank, Hans: Governor-general of Nazi-occupied Poland. Sentenced by West German court in 1945 to death by Nuremberg International Military Tribunal, hanged on October 16, 1946.

Franz, Kurt: SS sergeant in Treblinka. Sentenced in 1965 to life imprisonment.

Fritsch, Karl: Deputy commandant of Auschwitz. Died in May 1945.

Globocnik, Odilo: Builder and inspector general of Belzec, Sobibor, and Treblinka. Committed suicide by poison on June 6, 1945, to avoid arrest by British.

Goebbels, Joseph: Nazi minister of propaganda. Committed suicide in bunker underneath Berlin on May 1, 1945.

Göring, Hermann: Number-two man in the Nazi Party. Committed suicide in his cell at Nuremberg, October 15, 1946.

Heydrich, Reinhard: Head of the security police and the person assigned by Himmler to oversee the Final Solution. Died of wounds after ambush by Czech underground on June 5, 1942.

Himmler, Heinrich: Commander of the SS. Committed suicide at British interrogation center, May 23, 1945.

Hitler, Adolf: Supreme leader of Nazi Germany. Committed suicide in bunker beneath Berlin on April 30, 1945.

Höss, Rudolf: Commandant of Auschwitz-Birkenau. Hanged at Auschwitz in April 1947.

Hössler, Franz: SS captain in Auschwitz whose task was to calm new arrivals. Condemned to death by a British military court and executed on December 13, 1945.

Lambert, Herman: SS sergeant who headed a group of inmate builders in Treblinka.

Tried and acquitted after testimony from some of his former workers.

Mengele, Josef: Physician and one of chief selection officers in Auschwitz. Escaped to Brazil, where he supposedly suffered a stroke while swimming and was drowned in 1979. His remains were tentatively identified in 1985.

Mildner, Rudolf: SS colonel who served in Birkenau and also as the head of the State Police in Katowice, Poland. Tried and released in 1949.

Moll, Otto: Sergeant-major in the SS in charge of the gassing operation and later the cremations at Birkenau. Sentenced to death by American military court and executed on May 28, 1946.

Palitzsch, Gerhard: SS master sergeant whose specialty was shooting people in the back of the head. Fate after World War II unknown.

Stangl, Franz: Commandant of Treblinka. Escaped to Brazil, arrested there and extradited to Austria in 1979; sentenced to life imprisonment and died in prison shortly afterward.

Wirth, Christian: Head of the death camps in Poland. Believed to have been killed by Italian underground in May 1944.

The vast majority of the SS and Ukrainians who served in the death camps were never brought to trial.

Notes

Introduction: *Endlösung:*
The Final Solution

1. Quoted in Klaus P. Fischer, *Nazi Germany: A New History*. New York: Continuum, 1995, p. 168.

2. Quoted in Fischer, *Nazi Germany*, p. 169.

3. Quoted in Jeremy Noakes and Geoffrey Pridham, *Foreign Policy, War, and Racial Extermination*, vol. 3 of *Nazism, 1919–1945: A Documentary Reader*. Exeter, England: University of Exeter Press, 1988, p. 1,049.

4. Quoted in Yitzhak Arad, *Belzec, Sobibor, Treblinka*. Bloomington: Indiana University Press, 1987, p. 8.

5. Quoted in Fischer, *Nazi Germany*, p. 504.

6. Quoted in Rudolf Höss, Pery Broad, and Johann Paul Kremer, *KL Auschwitz Seen by the SS*, ed. Jadwiga Bezwinska and Danuta Czech, trans. Constantine Fitzgibbon, Krystyna Michalik, and Zbigniew Bezwinski. New York: Howard Fertig, 1984, p. 109.

7. Quoted in Arad, *Belzec, Sobibor, Treblinka*, p. 9.

8. Quoted in Samuel Willenberg, *Surviving Treblinka*, trans. Naftali Greenwood. Oxford: Basil Blackwell, 1989, p. 1.

Chapter 1: *Begrüsung:* The Welcome

9. Quoted in Willenberg, *Surviving Treblinka*, p. 11.

10. Quoted in Arad, *Belzec, Sobibor, Treblinka*, p. 63.

11. Quoted in Arad, *Belzec, Sobibor, Treblinka*, p. 64.

12. Quoted in Jadwiga Bezwinska and Danuta Czech, eds., *Amidst a Nightmare of Crime*, trans. Krystyna Michalik. Oświecim, Poland: State Museum at Oświecim, 1973, p. 90.

13. Olga Lengyel, *Five Chimneys: The Story of Auschwitz*. New York: Howard Fertig, 1983, p. 9.

14. Quoted in Otto Friedrich, *The Kingdom of Auschwitz*. New York: HarperCollins, 1992, p. 31.

15. Quoted in Lengyel, *Five Chimneys*, p. 8.

16. Quoted in Arad, *Belzec, Sobibor, Treblinka*, p. 63.

17. Quoted in Arad, *Belzec, Sobibor, Treblinka*, p. 169.

18. Quoted in Willenberg, *Surviving Treblinka*, p. 129.

19. Quoted in Noakes and Pridham, *Foreign Policy, War, and Racial Extermination*, p. 1,154.

20. Quoted in Noakes and Pridham, *Foreign Policy, War, and Racial Extermination*, p. 1,154.

21. Quoted in Friedrich, *The Kingdom of Auschwitz*, p. 20.

22. Quoted in Bezwinska and Czech, *Amidst a Nightmare of Crime*, p. 97.

23. Gisella Perl, *I Was a Doctor in Auschwitz*. New York: Arno Press, 1979, p. 27.

24. Quoted in Gerald L. Posner and John Ware, *Mengele: The Complete Story*. New York: McGraw-Hill, 1986, p. 19.

25. Quoted in Höss, Broad, and Kremer, *KL Auschwitz Seen by the SS*, p. 97.

26. Lengyel, *Five Chimneys*, p. 14.

27. Quoted in Arad, *Belzec, Sobibor, Treblinka*, p. 129.

28. Quoted in Filip Müller, *Eyewitness Auschwitz*, trans. Susanne Flatauer. New York: Stein and Day, 1979, p. 38.

29. Quoted in Arad, *Belzec, Sobibor, Treblinka*, p. 76.

30. Quoted in Müller, *Eyewitness Auschwitz*, p. 84.

31. Petro Mirchuk, *In the German Mills of Death, 1941–1945*. New York: Vantage Press, 1976, p. 61.

32. Elie Wiesel, *Night*. 1958. Reprinted New York: Avon Books, 1960, p. 40.

33. Quoted in Lengyel, *Five Chimneys*, p. 15.

34. Lengyel, *Five Chimneys*, p. 85.

35. Quoted in Müller, *Eyewitness Auschwitz*, p. 5.

36. Höss, Broad, and Kremer, *KL Auschwitz Seen by the SS*, p. 186.

37. Willenberg, *Surviving Treblinka*, p. 15.

38. Quoted in Willenberg, *Surviving Treblinka*, p. 50.

39. Willenberg, *Surviving Treblinka*, p. 25.

Chapter 2: *Sonderbehandlung:* Special Handling

40. Müller, *Eyewitness Auschwitz*, p. 44.

41. Quoted in Noakes and Pridham, *Foreign Policy, War, and Racial Extermination*, p. 1,141.

42. Quoted in Arad, *Belzec, Sobibor, Treblinka*, p. 9.

43. Quoted in Gerald Reitlinger, *The Final Solution*. South Brunswick, NY: Thomas Yoseloff, 1953, p. 154.

44. Quoted in Friedrich, *The Kingdom of Auschwitz*, p. 68.

45. Quoted in Müller, *Eyewitness Auschwitz*, p. 72.

46. Quoted in Arad, *Belzec, Sobibor, Treblinka*, p. 186.

47. Quoted in Noakes and Pridham, *Foreign Policy, War and Racial Extermination*, p. 1,151.

48. Quoted in Reitlinger, *The Final Solution*, p. 160.

49. Quoted in Reitlinger, *The Final Solution*, p. 161.

50. Quoted in Arad, *Belzec, Sobibor, Treblinka*, p. 71.

51. Müller, *Eyewitness Auschwitz*, p. 49.

52. Quoted in Willenberg, *Surviving Treblinka*, p. 18.

53. Quoted in Reitlinger, *The Final Solution*, p. 158.

54. Quoted in Müller, *Eyewitness Auschwitz*, p. 98.

55. Müller, *Eyewitness Auschwitz*, p. 138.

56. Willenberg, *Surviving Treblinka*, p. 53.

57. Perl, *I Was a Doctor in Auschwitz*, p. 66.

58. Quoted in Höss, Broad, and Kremer, *KL Auschwitz Seen by the SS*, p. 168.

59. Müller, *Eyewitness Auschwitz*, p. 52.

60. Lengyel, *Five Chimneys*, p. 85.

Chapter 3: *Arbeit Macht Frei:* Work Brings Freedom

61. Quoted in Bezwinska and Czech, *Amidst a Nightmare of Crime*, p. 185.

62. Mirchuk, *In the German Mills of Death*, p. 26.

63. Müller, *Eyewitness Auschwitz*, p. 97.

64. Quoted in Czeslaw Rajca and Anna Wisniewska, *Majdanek*, trans. Anna Zagorska. Lublin, Poland: State Museum of Majdanek, 1983, p. 53.

65. Quoted in Bezwinska and Czech, *Amidst a Nightmare of Crime*, p. 97.

66. Lengyel, *Five Chimneys*, p. 106.

67. Quoted in Lengyel, *Five Chimneys*, p. 32.

68. Quoted in Arad, *Belzec, Sobibor, Treblinka*, p. 137.

69. Quoted in Willenberg, *Surviving Treblinka*, p. 89.

70. Quoted in Bezwinska and Czech, *Amidst a Nightmare of Crime*, p. 99.

71. Quoted in Lengyel, *Five Chimneys*, p. 24.

72. Quoted in Rajca and Wisniewska, *Majdanek*, p. 19.

73. Friedrich, *The Kingdom of Auschwitz*, p. 68.

74. Perl, *I Was a Doctor in Auschwitz*, p. 38.

75. Mirchuk, *In the German Mills of Death*, p. 72.

76. Mirchuk, *In the German Mills of Death*, p. 35.

77. Quoted in Arad, *Belzec, Sobibor, Treblinka*, p. 233.

78. Quoted in Arad, *Belzec, Sobibor, Treblinka*, p. 79.

79. Quoted in Bezwinska and Czech, *Amidst a Nightmare of Crime*, p. 139.

80. Willenberg, *Surviving Treblinka*, p. 67.

81. Müller, *Eyewitness Auschwitz*, p. 29.

82. Quoted in Bezwinska and Czech, *Amidst a Nightmare of Crime*, p. 139.

83. Quoted in Rajca and Wisniewska, *Majdanek*, p. 57.

84. Quoted in Friedrich, *The Kingdom of Auschwitz*, p. 9.

85. Quoted in Arad, *Belzec, Sobibor, Treblinka*, p. 97.

86. Quoted in Friedrich, *The Kingdom of Auschwitz*, p. 39.

87. Müller, *Eyewitness Auschwitz*, p. 45.

88. Lengyel, *Five Chimneys*, p. 100.

Chapter 4: *Untermenschen:*
The Subhumans

89. Müller, *Eyewitness Auschwitz*, p. 103.

90. Quoted in Lengyel, *Five Chimneys*, p. 54.

91. Quoted in Friedrich, *The Kingdom of Auschwitz*, p. 85.

92. Quoted in Bezwinska and Czech, *Amidst a Nightmare of Crime*, p. 102.

93. Quoted in Arad, *Belzec, Sobibor, Treblinka*, p. 223.

94. Lengyel, *Five Chimneys*, p. 105.

95. Quoted in Arad, *Belzec, Sobibor, Treblinka*, p. 229.

96. Quoted in Arad, *Belzec, Sobibor, Treblinka*, p. 207.

97. Quoted in Bezwinska and Czech, *Amidst a Nightmare of Crime*, p. 136.

98. Willenberg, *Surviving Treblinka*, p. 48.

99. Quoted in Friedrich, *The Kingdom of Auschwitz*, p. 53.

100. Quoted in Willenberg, *Surviving Treblinka*, p. 67.

101. Quoted in Arad, *Belzec, Sobibor, Treblinka*, p. 216.

102. Quoted in Arad, *Belzec, Sobibor, Treblinka*, p. 216.

103. Wiesel, *Night*, p. 43.

104. Wiesel, *Night*, p. 80.

105. Lengyel, *Five Chimneys*, p. 110.

106. Perl, *I Was a Doctor in Auschwitz*, p. 79.

107. Willenberg, *Surviving Treblinka*, p. 58.

108. Müller, *Eyewitness Auschwitz*, p. 17.

109. Lengyel, *Five Chimneys*, p. 45.

110. Höss, Broad, and Kremer, *KL Auschwitz Seen by the SS*, p. 149.

111. Lengyel, *Five Chimneys*, p. 65.

Chapter 5: *Übermenschen:*
The Master Race

112. Reitlinger, *The Final Solution*, p. 127.

113. Quoted in Arad, *Belzec, Sobibor, Treblinka*, p. 68.

114. Jerzy Rawicz, foreword to Höss, Broad, and Kremer, *KL Auschwitz Seen by the SS*, p. 32.

115. Willenberg, *Surviving Treblinka*, p. 56.

116. Quoted in Arad, *Belzec, Sobibor, Treblinka*, p. 186.

117. Höss, Broad, and Kremer, *KL Auschwitz Seen by the SS*, p. 48.

118. Höss, Broad, and Kremer, *KL Auschwitz Seen by the SS*, p. 88.

119. Quoted in Arad, *Belzec, Sobibor, Treblinka*, p. 102.

120. Quoted in Noakes and Pridham, *Foreign Policy, War, and Racial Extermination*, p. 1,150.

121. Quoted in Bezwinska and Czech, *Amidst a Nightmare of Crime*, p. 38.

122. Quoted in Friedrich, *The Kingdom of Auschwitz*, p. 28.

123. Höss, Broad, and Kremer, *KL Auschwitz Seen by the SS*, p. 103.

124. Höss, Broad, and Kremer, *KL Auschwitz Seen by the SS*, p. 90.

125. Höss, Broad, and Kremer, *KL Auschwitz Seen by the SS*, p. 61.

126. Höss, Broad, and Kremer, *KL Auschwitz Seen by the SS*, p. 103.

127. Höss, Broad, and Kremer, *KL Auschwitz Seen by the SS*, p. 95.

128. Quoted in Arad, *Belzec, Sobibor, Treblinka*, p. 72.

129. Daniel Jonah Goldhagen, *Hitler's Willing Executioners*. New York: Knopf, 1996, p. 377.

130. Goldhagen, *Hitler's Willing Executioners*, p. 174.

131. Quoted in Müller, *Eyewitness Auschwitz*, p. 141.

132. Quoted in Arad, *Belzec, Sobibor, Treblinka*, p. 189.

133. Quoted in Arad, *Belzec, Sobibor, Treblinka*, p. 120.

134. Quoted in Müller, *Eyewitness Auschwitz*, p. 147.

135. Quoted in Posner and Ware, *Mengele*, p. 34.

136. Quoted in Posner and Ware, *Mengele*, p. 29.

137. Quoted in Noakes and Pridham, *Foreign Policy, War, and Racial Extermination*, p. 1,148.

138. Quoted in Müller, *Eyewitness Auschwitz*, p. 46.

139. Quoted in Posner and Ware, *Mengele*, p. 53.

140. Quoted in Arad, *Belzec, Sobibor, Treblinka*, p. 196.

141. Quoted in Friedrich, *The Kingdom of Auschwitz*, p. 23.

142. Quoted in Friedrich, *The Kingdom of Auschwitz*, p. 23.

143. Goldhagen, *Hitler's Willing Executioners*, p. 381.

Chapter 6: Escape, Rebellion, Liberation

144. Quoted in Arad, *Belzec, Sobibor, Treblinka*, p. 264.

145. Quoted in Arad, *Belzec, Sobibor, Treblinka*, p. 259.

146. Quoted in Arad, *Belzec, Sobibor, Treblinka*, p. 264.

147. Quoted in Arad, *Belzec, Sobibor, Treblinka*, p. 262.

148. Quoted in Bezwinska and Czech, *Amidst a Nightmare of Crime*, p. 116.

149. Quoted in Bezwinska and Czech, *Amidst a Nightmare of Crime*, p. 76.

150. Quoted in Arad, *Belzec, Sobibor, Treblinka*, p. 176.

151. Quoted in Arad, *Belzec, Sobibor, Treblinka*, p. 297.

152. Quoted in Arad, *Belzec, Sobibor, Treblinka*, p. 329.

153. Müller, *Eyewitness Auschwitz*, p. 156.

154. Quoted in Arad, *Belzec, Sobibor, Treblinka*, p. 343.

155. Quoted in Arad, *Belzec, Sobibor, Treblinka*, p. 345.

156. Quoted in Arad, *Belzec, Sobibor, Treblinka*, p. 347.

157. Quoted in Arad, *Belzec, Sobibor, Treblinka*, p. 359.

158. Friedrich, *The Kingdom of Auschwitz*, p. 71.

159. Quoted in Friedrich, *The Kingdom of Auschwitz*, p. 60.

160. Lengyel, *Five Chimneys*, p. 166.

161. Quoted in Friedrich, *The Kingdom of Auschwitz*, p. 74.

162. Quoted in Arad, *Belzec, Sobibor, Treblinka*, p. 371.

163. Quoted in Arad, *Belzec, Sobibor, Treblinka*, p. 371.

164. Lengyel, *Five Chimneys*, p. 197.

165. Quoted in Friedrich, *The Kingdom of Auschwitz*, p. 87.

166. Quoted in Friedrich, *The Kingdom of Auschwitz*, p. 90.

167. Quoted in Friedrich, *The Kingdom of Auschwitz*, p. 93.

Epilogue: "There Is No Why"

168. Quoted in Friedrich, *The Kingdom of Auschwitz*, p. 1.

169. Yehuda Bauer, *A History of the Holocaust*. New York: Franklin Watts, 1982, p. 1.

170. Ronnie S. Landau, *The Nazi Holocaust*. Chicago: Ivan R. Dee, 1992, p. 3.

171. Quoted in Goldhagen, *Hitler's Willing Executioners*, p. 394.

172. Quoted in Goldhagen, *Hitler's Willing Executioners*, p. 401.

173. Bauer, *A History of the Holocaust*, p. 336.

For Further Reading

David A. Adler, *Child of the Warsaw Ghetto.* New York: Holiday House, 1995. Fictional account of life in the Warsaw ghetto, the uprising against the Nazis, and imprisonment in Auschwitz told through the eyes of a Jewish boy. Excellent illustrations by Karen Ritz. For younger readers.

Lynda Atkinson, *In Kindling Flame: The Story of Hannah Senesh, 1921–1944.* New York: Lothrop, Lee & Shepard Books, 1985. The story of a young girl caught by the Nazis while attempting to rescue her fellow Jews in Hungary and subsequently executed.

Susan D. Bachrach, *Tell Them We Remember.* Boston: Little, Brown, 1994. Published for the U.S. Holocaust Memorial Museum. The entire story of the Holocaust, from the rise of the Nazis to the liberation of the concentration camps during World War II, told in short chapters liberally illustrated with photographs. Photographs of actual Holocaust victims and survivors are most touching.

Miriam Chaikin, *A Nightmare in History: The Holocaust, 1933–1945.* New York, Clarion Books, 1987. Short, easy-to-read account of the Holocaust interspersed with black-and-white photographs.

Gizelle Hersh and Peggy Mann, *Gizelle, Save the Children.* New York: Dodd, Mead, 1980. The recollections of a young girl who survived captivity in Auschwitz.

Barbara Rogasky, *Smoke and Ashes: The Story of the Holocaust.* New York: Holiday House, 1988. Excellent, comprehensive account of the Holocaust accompanied by black-and-white pictures. Good appendix on fate of top Nazis.

Richard Tames, *Nazi Germany.* London: Batsford Academic and Educational, 1985. A title in the Living Through History series. Short account of the Nazis' rise to power and mini-biographies of the leading Nazis and some of their opponents.

Works Consulted

Yitzhak Arad, *Belzec, Sobibor, Treblinka*. Bloomington: Indiana University Press, 1987. Excellent, comprehensive, and often shocking account of three of the death camps. Recommended for exceptional detail.

Yehuda Bauer, *A History of the Holocaust*. New York: Franklin Watts, 1982. One of the world's foremost authorities describes both the Holocaust and the events leading to it. Charts and maps help the reader get an accurate picture.

Jadwiga Bezwinska and Danuta Czech, eds., *Amidst a Nightmare of Crime*. Trans. Krystyna Michalik. Oświecim, Poland: State Museum at Oświecim, 1973. Eyewitness accounts—some written in the death camps, others in testimony at postwar trials—of surviving Auschwitz-Birkenau *Sonderkommando*.

Klaus P. Fischer, *Nazi Germany: A New History*. New York: Continuum, 1995. An excellent and complete overview of the roots of the Nazi Party, its rise to power, and its destruction.

Otto Friedrich, *The Kingdom of Auschwitz*. New York: HarperCollins, 1992. This short (103-page) paperback nevertheless conveys all the horror of Auschwitz-Birkenau.

Daniel Jonah Goldhagen, *Hitler's Willing Executioners*. New York: Knopf, 1996. Excellent study demonstrating that ordinary Germans, not only fanatical Nazis, were willing participants in the Holocaust.

Rudolf Höss, Pery Broad, and Johann Paul Kremer, *KL Auschwitz Seen by the SS*. Ed. Jadwiga Bezwinska and Danuta Czech. Trans. Constantine Fitzgibbon, Krystyna Michalik, and Zbignew Bezwinski. New York: Howard Fertig, 1984. Excerpts of the writings of three veteran SS officers give valuable insight into the mindset of those who worked in the death camps.

Ronnie S. Landau, *The Nazi Holocaust*. Chicago: Ivan R. Dee, 1992. Excellent overview of the Holocaust by the founding director of the British Holocaust Educational Project.

Olga Lengyel, *Five Chimneys: The Story of Auschwitz*. New York: Howard Fertig, 1983. Extremely moving account of the author's experiences as a doctor in a death camp. Does not reveal the big picture, but the collection of little pictures is just as valuable.

Petro Mirchuk, *In the German Mills of Death, 1941–1945*. New York: Vantage Press, 1976. The author, who survived as a death camp prisoner from the summer of 1942 until the end of World War II, gives a fascinating account of his experiences.

Filip Müller, *Eyewitness Auschwitz*. Trans. Susanne Flatauer. New York: Stein and Day, 1979. Excellent, disturbing account of life and death in Auschwitz-Birkenau by a survivor of the *Sonderkommando*.

Jeremy Noakes and Geoffrey Pridham, *Foreign Policy, War, and Racial Extermination*. Vol. 3 of *Nazism, 1919–1945: A Documentary Reader*. Exeter, England: University of Exeter Press, 1988. The story of the Holocaust is told in quotations from speeches, letters, and other documents by the participants, both perpetrators and victims.

Gisella Perl, *I Was a Doctor in Auschwitz*. New York: Arno Press, 1979. Excellent, firsthand look at life in a death camp from the author's remarkable perspective.

Gerald L. Posner and John Ware, *Mengele: The Complete Story*. New York: McGraw-Hill, 1986. Comprehensive biography of the SS doctor in Auschwitz-Birkenau. The focus on his time in the death camp is relatively brief.

Czeslaw Rajca and Anna Wisniewska, *Majdanek*. Trans. Anna Zagorska. Lublin, Poland: State Museum of Majdanek, 1983. Lengthy introduction relating the history of the camp is followed by numerous short recollections by survivors.

Gerald Reitlinger, *The Final Solution*. South Brunswick, NY: Thomas Yoseloff, 1953. One of the earliest and best attempts to document and explain the Holocaust, the tragedy of which is not lost in the mass of details.

William L. Shirer, *The Rise and Fall of the Third Reich*. New York: Simon & Schuster, 1959. Written by an award-winning journalist, this is one of the most comprehensive and readable of the histories of Nazi Germany.

Louis L. Snyder, *Encyclopedia of the Third Reich*. New York: Paragon House, 1989. An indispensable tool for anyone studying Nazi Germany. All the major people, places, and events are described in short articles in alphabetical order.

John Weiss, *Ideology of Death: Why the Holocaust Happened in Germany*. Chicago: Ivan R. Dee, 1996. Explores the course of history in Germany and Austria and the character of their people in order to explain the Holocaust.

Elie Wiesel, *Night*. 1958. Reprinted New York: Avon Books, 1960. Personal recollections of his experiences in Auschwitz by a winner of the Nobel Peace Prize.

Samuel Willenberg, *Surviving Treblinka*. Trans. Naftali Greenwood. Oxford: Basil Blackwell, 1989. Eyewitness account of one of the death camps by a surviving *Sonderkommando* worker.

Leni Yahil, *The Holocaust: The Fate of European Jewry*. Trans. Ina Friedman and Haya Galai. Oxford: Oxford University Press, 1990. One of the most complete accounts of the Holocaust from a Jewish perspective. Details of the death camps are limited.

Index

Picture Credits

Cover photo: Corbis-Bettmann

AP/Wide World Photos, 21, 40, 41, 69, 87

Archive Photos, 37, 46

Archive Photos/DPA, 53

Archive Photos/Hackett, 27

Bildarchiv Preussischer Kulterbesitz, courtesy of the Simon Wiesenthal Center Library and Archives, 49

Corbis-Bettmann, 75

Dachau Concentration Camp Memorial, courtesy of the Simon Wiesenthal Center Library and Archives, 64

Dokumentationsarchiv des Osterreichisechen Widerstandes, courtesy of USHMM Photo Archives, 15

Jerzy Ficowski, courtesy of USHMM Photo Archives, 16

Sidney Harcsztark, courtesy of USHMM Photo Archives, 19

KZ Gedenkstatte Dachau, courtesy of USHMM Photo Archives, 47, 92

Library of Congress, 44

Main Commission for the Investigation of Nazi War Crimes, courtesy of USHMM Photo Archives, 26, 33, 35, 63, 68, 76, 90

National Archives, 28, 39, 78, 91, 95

National Archives, courtesy of USHMM Photo Archives, 14, 58

Peter Newark's Historical Pictures, 67, 70

Rijksinstituut voor Oorlogsdocumentatie, courtesy of USHMM Photo Arhcives, 72

Robert A. Schmuhl, courtesy of USHMM Photo Archives, 43

State Museum of Auschwitz-Birkenau, courtesy of USHMM Photo Archives, 24, 51

UPI/Corbis-Bettmann, 11, 29, 48, 54, 57, 88

Yad Vashem Photo Archives, courtesy of USHMM Photo Archives, 50, 80, 84

YIVO Institute for Jewish Research, courtesy of USHMM Photo Archives, 32

Roberta Zuckerman, courtesy of USHMM Photo Archives, 83

About the Author

William W. Lace is a native of Fort Worth, Texas. He holds a bachelor's degree from Texas Christian University, a master's from East Texas State University, and a doctorate from the University of North Texas. After working for newspapers in Baytown, Texas, and Forth Worth, he joined the University of Texas at Arlington as sports information director and later became the director of the news service. He is now director of college relations for the Tarrant County Junior College District in Fort Worth. He and his wife, Laura, live in Arlington and have two children. Lace has written one other book in the Holocaust Library, *The Nazis*.